A LOVER SINGS

A Lover Sings
Selected Lyrics

BILLY BRAGG

ff

FABER & FABER

This edition first published in the UK in 2015 by
Faber & Faber Ltd
Bloomsbury House
74–77 Great Russell Street
London WC1B 3DA

Typeset by Hamish Ironside
Printed in Germany by GGP Media GmbH, Pößneck

A CIP record for this book is available from the British Library

ISBN 978-0-571-32859-8

10 9 8 7 6 5 4 3 2

To J & J

Contents

Introduction

I learned to play guitar when I was sixteen, but I'd been string-ing words together since I was twelve years old. Like most kids, I was encouraged to write poetry at school, but unlike the rest of my classmates, I never gave up. A poem I wrote for homework caught the eye of my English teacher, and when I was chosen to read it out on local radio, I got this crazy idea that I was a poet. Some of my early efforts were attempts at poetry, but soon I was thinking up tunes to go with my words, although the fact that I couldn't play an instrument meant that I had to keep the melodies in my head.

Over the summer of 1974, my schooldays kind of petered out. Not expecting much joy from my exam results and unenthused about looking for a job, I was hoping something else might come along. Through the wall of our back room, I heard the kid next door playing his electric guitar. It was the sound of salvation. Wiggy was two years younger than me and obsessed with the Faces. Soon he was teaching me how to play my way through the Rod Stewart songbook he'd bought on mail order. There's a great picture of the two of us from this period, strumming our guitars in his back garden. We're both playing completely different chords, but we're doing so with great intent.

Learning to play guitar gave a huge boost to my song-writing and I began to fill notebooks with page after page of lyrics that were mostly derived from whichever artist I was infatuated with at the time. I first started to really listen to the words of the songs on the radio after hearing 'The Boxer' by Simon and Garfunkel in 1970. I remember poring over Paul Simon's lyrics on the back of the *Bridge over Troubled Water* LP sleeve. That album provided me with a gateway into the singer-songwriter genre, but the production values were so high, I was unable to figure out how the songs were constructed. Then, at age fifteen, somebody played me Bob Dylan's *Greatest Hits*, a collection of songs from his first seven albums. I was immediately drawn to the starker, solo material, which, although less than a decade old when I first heard it, sounded like it came from a hundred years ago. Not only were songs like 'Blowin' in the Wind', 'The Times They Are a-Changin'' and 'Mr Tambourine Man' easy to deconstruct – most utilising no more than three chords – they also carried a message. It was this material that provided the template for my early song-writing.

My other obsession at the time was the pop soul of the Motown label. They regularly produced compilations of their hits, which I avidly sought out. *Motown Chartbusters Volume 3* might just be the greatest pop album ever released. It contains, among other gems, 'I Heard It Through the Grapevine', 'Dancing in the Street' and 'Roadrunner', and it climaxes – chronologically and emotionally – with 'The Tracks of My Tears'. It was this last track that really caught my attention. Like Dylan, Smokey Robinson needed no more than three chords to create a masterpiece. I duly took note.

Although the household I grew up in was apolitical, the music that I listened to was full of opinions. Simon and Garfunkel, Dylan and the other singer-songwriters were always asking questions, but the politics of the '60s ran deeply through soul music too. On *Motown Chartbusters Volume 5*, Smokey's 'Tears of a Clown' is followed by Edwin Starr's 'War'. Next, a teen pop interlude with the Jackson 5 gives way to the Temptations' 'Ball of Confusion' – an angry four minutes of funky WTF.

The starkest transition is from the infectious joy of the Supremes' 'Stoned Love' to Marvin Gaye's solemn, string-backed reading of 'Abraham, Martin and John'. This latter song, reflecting on the assassinations of Abraham Lincoln, John Kennedy, Martin Luther King and Robert Kennedy, could hardly qualify as a chartbuster, never having been released as a single prior to appearing on this album. It was presumably included in the collection by way of an explanation for the change of tone that had overcome Motown's prodigious pop output since the last volume of *Chartbusters*. It was from these records that I began to first pick up my politics.

During this period, my songwriting technique was pretty rudimentary. I don't know how others perfected their skills, but I did it by replacing the lyrics of my favourite songs with rhymes of my own. These were songs that I'd heard many times over, the nuanced phrasings and internal rhythms so familiar to me that, when I came to place my own words there, they fitted seamlessly into the tune.

In this way, I was able to become a songwriter without any knowledge of the principles of music. I had friends who could read the crotchets and quavers, but the five staff lines that they were hung from seemed to act like train tracks, taking them up and down the same lines every day, like commuters governed by a rigid timetable. Music is all about feel and you just can't write that stuff down. To this day, I play by ear because I don't want to have to think about anything but the words.

Soon, Wiggy and I had found other wayward souls willing to lug their drum kits, keyboards or bass cabinets round to our house and happily play along with tunes we'd written. It didn't matter that our songs sounded similar to those whose records we incessantly played on our cheap turntables. These artists were our heroes and our imitation was not intended as flattery, but was instead an attempt to momentarily close the vast distances between us.

It took a revolutionary movement to shake me from my reliance on the music of the past. I was nineteen when punk rock happened, of the same generation as Joe Strummer and Johnny Rotten, and this sudden shock of the now gave me the confidence to write in the style of my contemporaries. Punk rock injected my songwriting with urgency and attitude and helped me to find my voice, yet it would be another two years before I wrote what I considered to be my first Billy Bragg song.

To get to that place, I first had to expunge the influences that had shaped my writing: all those singer-songwriter albums had to go, as well as the *Motown Chartbusters*. I also had to bid farewell to the traditional English folk artists whose albums I had brought home many times from the public library – the Watersons, Shirley and Dolly Collins, Ewan MacColl. Punk rock was Year Zero and I was now under the influence of writers with attitude like Elvis Costello, Paul Weller and the Ramones.

By 1977, Wiggy and I had found a fellow traveller in drummer Robert Handley and, with an ever-rotating line-up of bass players, we had graduated from playing in back rooms to doing gigs under the name Riff Raff. I still had pages in my notebooks where ideas tailed off after a few rhyming couplets, but, more often than not, I was finishing songs and the band were immediately connecting with them. Riff Raff had a good-time, roustabout style, and I wrote songs that played to our strengths.

When the band ran out of steam in 1980, so did my song-writing. Without the regular stimulus of performance, the need to write new songs left me and I began to think I'd missed my chance to make a go of being a musician. Having run out of options, I attempted to press the eject button on my previous existence by joining the army, but perversely, the experience only inspired me to start writing songs again.

Extricating myself from the Royal Armoured Corps, I began formulating a plan whereby I would utilise the vulnerability of the singer-songwriter and mix it with the angry attitude of punk rock. To do this, I needed a new kind of material; short, sharp songs delivered in a choppy, percussive style that ran contrary to the traditional image of the solo singer-songwriter strumming an acoustic guitar and playing ballads.

By the early '80s, punk rock had been superseded by the new romantics, and synthesiser duos were all the rage. My intention was to zig while the music scene was zagging and, in doing so, pick up some of those who, appalled by Spandau Ballet and their insistence on style over content, yearned for the fire of punk.

If I hoped to stand out in such a crowd, the dynamics of my new material would be almost as important as the melodies. I began building songs around guitar riffs – 'The Milkman of Human Kindness' relies on an alternating low/high attack; 'To Have and to Have Not' is all punchy chords; 'Richard', a favourite from the Riff Raff set, was retooled with the addition of some jarring open-string notes; and 'A New England' went from a tune played in ringing tones to a chugging bass-string pulse.

As I became more confident, my early influences began to seep back into my songwriting. A Paul Simon lyric would be referenced or a Bob Dylan tune borrowed, allowing the listener to see my back pages. Performing at benefit gigs during the 1984 miners' strike, my love of folk music was reawakened when I found myself sharing the bill with traditional singers whose repertoire was far more radical than mine. And as the production of my albums became more elaborate, I enjoyed drawing on the sound of the soul records that I had loved as a teen. Having found my own voice, this was my way of owning up to the debt I owed to those whose tunes had inspired my earliest efforts.

I was fortunate in that my breakthrough in 1983–4 coincided with a resurgence in the art of songwriting. The emergence of first the Smiths and then the Pogues brought the focus sharply back onto lyrical content. Words began to matter again and pop had a moment akin to the '60s boom in kitchen-sink dramas. For a while, songs of social realism featured regularly on *Top of the Pops*, in between all the usual light entertainment.

My reputation as a protest singer stems from this period. These were politically charged times, and my songwriting reflected the struggles that were going on, not only on the picket lines, but also in the bedroom. Yes, some of my material was purely polemical, but even in the most tender of my love songs, a character is likely to make a passing political reference. Back then it felt like our personal relationships were shaped by the politics of the time.

And while I've never shied away from the label 'protest singer', I like to think my personal songs are just as powerful as my polemics and long ago stopped worrying about striking a balance between the two. Whether you're lovelorn or radical, I'm just trying to help you make sense of the world, because that's what my favourite songs did for me.

Smokey Robinson made me feel like I wasn't the only person who has ever had their heart broken and the Clash made me realise that I was not alone in my opposition to discrimination. Music has the ability to draw us out of isolation and connect us with a greater community where we feel that our troubles and concerns are recognised and shared. A song that is sympathetic to your mood can be therapeutic, the melody soothing while the words summon up feelings that you may not be able to easily articulate.

To be in a crowd of strangers at a concert, singing along to a favourite song, provides a collective experience rarely encountered in modern daily life. Individuality melts away and emotions become communal. For a few minutes, everyone in the space shares a common purpose – to sing the song at the top of their voice. If music has any real power, it lies in this moment, when we experience the solidarity of song, the cathartic realisation that you're not the only person who shares the sentiments that are being so forcefully expressed.

In the early '90s, I got together with my long-term partner, Juliet, and in 1993, my own perspective on everything was changed by the birth of our son, which gave me an unimpeachable reason to step back from ten years of being 'Billy Bragg'. The songs on the first post-baby album, *William Bloke*, were more personal, less ideological, but so was the world that our son was born into. The Cold War had ended, Thatcher was gone and pop culture was in a celebratory mood. Politics was passé; it was time to dance.

I was wondering what protest singers did when they were no longer fashionable when I got a call from Woody Guthrie's daughter. Would I be interested in writing some new music for Woody's lost lyrics? The opportunity to collaborate with the original protest singer was too good to pass up. Before she allowed me to wade through the 2,000-plus lyrics in the archives, Nora Guthrie made it clear to me that she wanted a record that countered the image of her father as the saintly singer of worthy songs. Woody had been an iconoclast and Wilco and I were hired to help him down from the shiny pedestal that pop mythology had placed him on.

Wading through the boxes of manuscript lyrics in the archive gave me a fresh view of the role of the songwriter. Woody never wrote a cynical song in his life – he hated songs that made ordinary people feel they were worthless. Reading his words, I came to see cynicism as the true enemy of all of us who wish to create a fairer society and vowed to keep mine in check.

But the biggest lesson came from Nora. She felt that the deification of her father had robbed his work of its ability to challenge America's image of itself. She was looking to cast out the myth of Woody Guthrie and force people to see the man as he really was: an ornery Okie, full of annoying con-tradictions and unexpected depths. When, in the early years of the twenty-first century, the neo-fascist British National Party began to win seats on local councils, Nora's example gave me the courage to challenge the perceptions of my own audience.

I've long believed that the role of the artist is not to lead the people, but to be a signpost that points the way ahead.

But what do you do if you believe that the people should be heading towards a territory they are unfamiliar with, one that makes them feel uncomfortable just talking about? Due to their commitment to internationalism, British leftists have traditionally avoided any discussion of identity politics. To talk about nationalism was taboo; to appear patriotic was heresy.

When the BNP began winning in Labour's traditional strongholds in England, it became increasingly clear that this squeamishness was having a negative effect. By refusing to address the issue of Englishness, the left had created a vacuum which gave the BNP free rein to decide who did and who didn't belong in England.

While I shared the left's commitment to internationalism, I'd always had a strong sense of my own identity and being English played a part of that. The England that I loved was one of the most multicultural societies in Europe, and I saw that as a bulwark against the fascists, if only we could find the gumption to stick a St George's flag onto it.

My first attempt to articulate that idea was the song 'England, Half English' which ends with me saying 'Oh my country, what a beautiful country you are'. The first time I played it live, an old comrade asked, 'You're being ironic, right?' His shocked reaction when I told him I was being serious convinced me that it is sometimes more constructive to challenge the beliefs of your audience than constantly re-inforce them. I don't accept accusations of 'preaching to the converted' – just like everyone else, activists need their spirits lifted by the solidarity of song – but I do relish those moments when I know my lyrics are taking the audience out of their comfort zone.

By far the biggest change since I began writing songs has been the digitisation of music. Where once it would take an age to get a topical song released – the miners' strike had ended before 'Between the Wars' hit the shops – I can now write, record and post a song on the Internet, to be heard around the world in a matter of minutes.

That same technology allows teenagers to comment about the world without having to first learn to write songs, play guitar or do gigs as I had to. I'm glad about that, because it means more people are able to make a contribution, but songwriting is of a different stripe to posting your views online. It has taken me around the world and given me the chance to experience cultures other than my own, challenging me to raise my game to reach different audiences.

Performing my songs night after night while trying my best to engage with those people out there in the dark has taught me that, while music has power, it doesn't have agency. Singing songs won't change the world, no matter how much we might want it to. Music can bring us together in common cause, engage and inspire us, focus our anger, and raise funds and awareness, but ultimately the only people with the ability to bring about real change are in the audience, not on stage. Tomorrow, the singer will be gone, bringing his or her music to another town, but those who were in the audience will still be there, having to face up to the challenges of their environment.

If the singer has helped recharge their activism, if the songs that were sung have made them feel they are not alone in their struggle, then that is probably about as much as music can do. And although I fully recognise that it's a small contribution in the overall scope of things, I keep faith in the ability of music to make a difference.

DORSET
AUGUST 2015

A LOVER SINGS

Cosmonaut

5–4–3–2–1

I wanna be a cosmonaut
I wanna be a cosmonaut
I wanna be a cosmonaut
I wanna be a cosmonaut

I should be starring
Just like Gagarin
There's the place for me

I could be flying
A super Vostock
For the CCCP

What can you hope to gain
Hanging around the Ukraine
Soviet fortune and fame
You know they don't have rock'n'roll in Moscow

Everybody's certain
Behind the Iron Curtain
That the West is inferior

Let me tell you comrade
By next Lenin's birthday
I'll be famous in Siberia

I wanna be a star in the USSR
I wanna be a hero in the Soviet Union

The Milkman of Human Kindness

If you are lonely, I will call
If you are poorly, I will send poetry

I love you
I am the milkman of human kindness
I will leave an extra pint

If you are sleeping, I will wait
If your bed is wet, I will dry your tears

Hold my hand for me I'm waking up
Hold my hand for me I'm waking up
Won't you hold my hand – I'm making up
Hold my hand for me I'm making up

If you are falling, I'll put out my hands
If you feel bitter, I will understand

To Have and to Have Not

Up in the morning and out to school
Mother says there'll be no work next year
Qualifications once the golden rule
Are now just pieces of paper

Just because you're better than me
Doesn't mean I'm lazy
Just because you're going forwards
Doesn't mean I'm going backwards

If you look the part you'll get the job
In last year's trousers and your old school shoes
The truth is, son, it's a buyer's market
They can afford to pick and choose

Just because you're better than me
Doesn't mean I'm lazy
Just because I dress like this
Doesn't mean I'm a communist

The factories are closing and the army's full
I don't know what I'm going to do
But I've come to see in the Land of the Free
There's only a future for the chosen few

At twenty-one you're on top of the scrap heap
At sixteen you were top of your class
All they taught you at school
Was how to be a good worker
The system has failed you, don't fail yourself

Richard

Richard belongs to Jayne
And Jayne belongs to yesterday
How can I go on
When every alpha particle hides a neon nucleus?

Neil belongs to love
And love belongs to no man
How can he go on
When no one answers the adverts in his mind?

There will be parties, there will be fun
There will be prizes for everyone
And hey, hey, hey, here comes Richard
There will be ladies dressed in lace
I just want to see her face
When hey, hey, hey, here comes Richard

You helped me build this bed
But you won't help me sleep in it
When I fall between you and the wall
Our titanic love affair sails on the morning tide

I really love your style
Did you read it in the *Look and Learn*?
How long can we go on?
Do you think I only love you
Because you sleep with other boys?

A New England

I was twenty-one years when I wrote this song
I'm twenty-two now, but I won't be for long
People ask me, 'When will you grow up to be a man?'
But all the girls I loved at school are already pushing prams

I loved you then as I love you still
Though I put you on a pedestal, they put you on the pill
I don't feel bad about letting you go
I just feel sad about letting you know

I don't want to change the world
I'm not looking for a new England
I'm just looking for another girl

I loved the words you wrote to me
But that was bloody yesterday
I can't survive on what you send
Every time you need a friend

I saw two shooting stars last night
I wished on them but they were only satellites
Is it wrong to wish on space hardware?
I wish, I wish, I wish you'd care

The Man in the Iron Mask

When he drops you off, I will not say
'Who was that who so quickly drove away?'
The things you've done and the places you've been
When I open the door for you
I will not let them in

As long as you come back to me
I will never ask
For you I will be
The Man in the Iron Mask

You said you loved me and it broke my heart
I was always your prisoner right from the start
The nights you spend without me
This house is like a dungeon
And you only return to torture me more

You must have your reasons
I will not ask
For you I will be
The Man in the Iron Mask

The Busy Girl Buys Beauty

The busy girl buys beauty
The pretty girl buys style
And the simple girl buys
What she's told to buy
And sees her world
Through the brightly lit eyes
Of the glossy romance of fashion
Where she can learn
Top tips for the gas cook
Successful secrets of a sexual kind
The daily drill for beautiful hair
And the truth about pain

What was Anna Ford wearing?
What did Angela Rippon say?
What will you do
When you wake up one morning
To find that God's made you plain
In a beautiful person's world?
And all those quick recipes
Have let you down
And you're twenty and a half, and not yet engaged
Will you go look for the boy who says
'I love you – let's get married and have kids'?

The busy girl buys beauty
The pretty girl buys style
And the simple girl buys
What she's told to buy
And sees her world
Through the brightly lit eyes

Of the glossy romance of fashion
Where she can learn
Top tips for the gas cook
Successful secrets of a sexual kind
The daily drill for beautiful hair
In a mail order paradise

Lover's Town Revisited

It's that summer of the evening
Get ready and roll the cassette
There's boys outside preaching genocide
And trying to think up some sort of threat
And the ladies in the cloakroom
Take no notice of me
I wish myself was back at home
But there's nothing safe in watching TV

There's something born tomorrow
That I lost when I was out for a drink
How many gangs is it gonna take
To change the way I think?
It takes more than good intentions
And a big bloke on the door
Though it's never the same after the first time
That doesn't stop them coming back for more

Fighting in the dance halls happens anyway
Sometimes it makes me stop and think
Sometimes it makes me turn away
Sometimes it makes me stop and think
Sometimes it makes me turn away
Sometimes it makes me stop and think
But most times it makes me run away

It Says Here

It says here that the unions will never learn
It says here that the economy is on the upturn
And it says here we should be proud that we are free
And our free press reflects our democracy
Those braying voices on the right of the House
Are echoed down the Street of Shame
Where politics mix with bingo and tits
In a money and numbers game

Where they offer you a feature
On stockings and suspenders
Next to a call for stiffer penalties for sex offenders

It says here that this year's prince is born
It says here, 'Do you ever wish that you were better informed?'
And it says here that we can only stop the rot
With a large dose of law and order and a touch of the short
    sharp shock

If this does not reflect your view you should understand
Those who own the papers also own this land
And they'd rather you believed
In Coronation Street capers
In the war of circulation, it sells newspapers
Could it be an infringement
Of the freedom of the press
To print pictures of women in states of undress?

When you wake up to the fact
That your paper is Tory
Just remember, there are two sides to every story

The Myth of Trust

I woke up this morning
To find that we have outlived the myth of trust
You woke up this morning
To the fact we've lost the things
We took for granted between us
Because I grew up in awe of the girl next door
And the boy that never cried
I was dreaming of those Elizabethan girls
While you were working in the market
To earn ourselves
And when you found out what happened yesterday
While you were away in this land of Cain
We were upstairs in the bedroom
Dancing disgusting
And flushing our babies down the drain
And the apple that don't wanna get eaten
Will still fall off the tree
When you're in as deep as we are, honey
It's so easy to get washed out to sea
For the facts of life are not man and wife
But Man and Woman sadly
And the apple that doesn't want to get eaten
Will still fall off the tree

I woke up this morning
To find that we have outlived the myth of trust

From a Vauxhall Velox

She said, 'Do these seats fold down?'
And I said, 'If you pull that handle'
All the time she'd been waiting for
Something with a little more
And all her mates on the new estates
Were walking out in confetti and sunshine

Her mother read her mail
And her dad was a policeman
Which I must say worried me
But some things have just got to be
So we passed very fast like ships in the night
Or cars in a contraflow system

Some people say love is blind
And I think that's just a bit short-sighted
Some people just want it now
It doesn't matter where or how
Satisfaction takes a second place
So long as they can get excited

The Saturday Boy

I'll never forget the first day I met her
That September morning was clear and fresh
The way she spoke and laughed at my jokes
And the way she rubbed herself against the edge of my desk

She became a magic mystery to me
And we'd sit together in double history twice a week
And some days we'd walk the same way home
And it's surprising how quick a little rain can clear the streets

We dreamed of her and compared our dreams
But that was all that I ever tasted
'Cos she lied to me with her body, you see
I lied to myself 'bout the chances I'd wasted

The times we were close
Were far and few between
In the darkness at the dances in the school canteen
Did she close her eyes as I did
When we held each other tight?
And *la la la la la la la la la means I love you*

She danced with me and I still hold that memory soft and sweet
And I stare up at her window as I walk down her street
But I never made the first team, I just made the first team laugh
And she never came to the phone, she was always in the bath

In the end it took me a dictionary
To find out the meaning of unrequited
While she was giving herself for free
At a party to which I was never invited

I never understood my failings then
And I hide my humble hopes now
Thinking back she made us want her
A girl not old enough to shave her legs

Island of No Return

Digging all day and digging all night
To keep my foxhole out of sight
Digging into dinner on a plate on my knees
The smell of damp webbing in the morning breeze
Fear in my stomach, fear in the sky
I eat my dinner with a weary eye
After all this it won't be the same
Messing around on Salisbury Plain

Pick up your feet, fall in, move out
We're going to a party way down south
Me and the Corporal out on a spree
Damned from here to eternity
I can already taste the blood in my mouth
Going to a party way down south

I hate this flat land, there's no cover
For sons and fathers and brothers and lovers
I can take the killing, I can take the slaughter
But I don't talk to *Sun* reporters
I never thought that I would be
Fighting fascists in the Southern Sea
I saw one today and in his hand
Was a weapon that was made in Birmingham

I wish Kipling and the Captain were here
To record our pursuits for posterity
Me and the Corporal out on a spree
Damned from here to eternity

St Swithin's Day

Thinking back now
I suppose you were just stating your views
What was it all for?
For the weather or the Battle of Agincourt?
And the times that we all hoped would last
Like a train they have gone by so fast
And though we stood together
At the edge of the platform
We were not moved by them

With my own hands
When I make love to your memory
It's not the same
I miss the thunder
I miss the rain
And the fact that you don't understand
Casts a shadow over this land
But the sun still shines from behind it

Thanks all the same
But I just can't bring myself to answer your letters
It's not your fault
But your honesty touches me like a fire
The Polaroids that hold us together
Will surely fade away
Like the love that we spoke of forever
On St Swithin's Day

A Lover Sings

You and I are victims of a love
That lost a lot in the translation
When I think of all the time that I spent
Sitting on the end of your bed in anticipation
Of you giving in and us living in sin

A hot day, the smell of hairspray
And the sound of a shower running softly
It's things like this that remind me how I felt
The first time you came back for coffee
The way you took it amazed me

Walking in the park, kissing in the dark
And my head against your pillow
And late at night a lover sings
Adam and Eve are finding out all about love
I say Adam and Eve are finding out all about love

There is no real substitute
For a ball struck squarely and firmly
And you're the kind of girl who wants to
Open up the bottle of pop too early in the journey
Our love went flat, just like that

It doesn't matter the colour of the car
But what goes on beneath the bonnet
Is there a flag that flies above your heart?
And is my name writ there upon it?
Wedding cake and toothache equals love and pain

Walking in the park, kissing on the carpet
And your tights around your ankles
And late at night a lover thinks of these things
Adam and Eve are finding out all about love
I say Adam and Eve are finding out all about love
Adam and Eve are finding out all about
Adam and Eve are finding out all about
Teresa and Steve are finding out all about love

Between the Wars

I was a miner, I was a docker
I was a railwayman between the wars
I raised a family in time of austerity
With sweat at the foundry between the wars

I paid the union and as times got harder
I looked to the government to help the working man
But they brought prosperity down at the armoury
We're arming for peace, me boys, between the wars

I kept the faith and I kept voting
Not for the iron fist but for the helping hand
For theirs is a land with a wall around it
And mine is a faith in my fellow man

Theirs is a land of hope and glory
Mine is the green field and the factory floor
Theirs are the skies all dark with bombers
And mine is the peace we knew between the wars

Call up the craftsmen, bring me the draughtsmen
Build me a path from cradle to grave
And I'll give my consent to any government
That does not deny a man a living wage

Go find the young men never to fight again
Bring up the banners from the days gone by
Sweet moderation, heart of this nation
Desert us not, we are between the wars

I Don't Need This Pressure, Ron

What was that bang? It was the next big thing
Exploding over our heads
And soon the next generation
Will emerge from behind the bike sheds
What are we going to offer them?
The exact same thing as before
But a different way to wear it
And the promise of a whole lot more

Oh, pity the pressures at the top
The tantrums and the tears
And the sound of platinum cash tills
Ringing in their ears
Money maketh man a Tory
Don't fire that assumption at me
I like toast as much as anyone
But not for breakfast, dinner and tea

So don't saddle me with your ideals
And spare me all your guilt
For a poet with all the answers
Has never yet been built

I see no shame in putting my name
To socialism's cause
Or seeking some more relevance
Than spotlight and applause
Neither in the name of conscience
Nor the name of charity
Money is put where mouths are
In the name of solidarity

We sing of freedom
And we speak of liberation
But such chances come
But once a generation
So I'll ignore what I am sure
Were the best of your intentions
You are judged by your actions
And not by your pretensions

There is drudgery in social change
And glory for the few
And if you don't tell me what not to say
I won't tell you what not to do

Scholarship Is the Enemy of Romance

Scholarship is the enemy of romance
Where does that leave me? Alone in the rain again
What happened to the weekend I planned with you?
We didn't even get upstairs this time

I never missed that end-of-term kiss
But where did it go, miss? I don't know, miss

Take me to the fair and hold me close as we fly through the air
Then suddenly on Sunday, it all just melted away
And when it had gone, between patches of yellowing grass
I found a coin and lost what I was looking for

I never took the advice in that book
Oh you should look, sir, you might learn, sir
You might learn, sir

Walk Away Renée (Version)

She said it was just a figment of speech
And I said, 'You mean figure?'
And she said, 'No, figment'
Because she could never imagine it happening
But it did

When we first met I played the shy boy
And when she spoke to me for the first time
My nose began to bleed
She guessed the rest

The next day we went on a bus ride to the ferry
And when nobody came to collect our fares
Well, I knew then this was something special
I couldn't stop thinking about her
And every time I switched on the radio
There was somebody else singing a song about the two of us
It was just like being on a fast ride at the funfair
The sort you wanna get off because it's scary
And then as soon as you're off
You wanna get straight back on again

But, oh, love is strange
And you have to take the crunchy with the smooth I s'pose
She began going out with Mr Potato Head
It was when I saw her in the car park
With his coat around her shoulders that I realised
I went home and thought about the two of them together
Until the bath water went cold around me
I thought about her eyes and the curve of her breasts
And about the point where their bodies met

I confronted her about it
I said, 'I'm the most illegible bachelor in town'
And she said, 'Yeah, that's why I can never understand
Any of those silly letters you send me'

And then one day it happened
She cut her hair and I stopped loving her

Greetings to the New Brunette (aka Shirley)

Shirley
It's quite exciting to be sleeping here in this new room
Shirley
You're my reason to get out of bed before noon
Shirley
You know when we sat out on the fire escape talking
Shirley
What did you say about running before we were walking?

Sometimes when we're as close as this
It's like we're in a dream
How can you lie there and think of England
When you don't even know who's in the team?

Shirley
Your sexual politics has left me all of a muddle
Shirley
We are joined in the ideological cuddle

I'm celebrating my love for you
With a pint of beer and a new tattoo
And if you haven't noticed yet
I'm more impressionable when my cement is wet

Politics and pregnancy
Are debated as we empty our glasses
And how I love those evening classes

Shirley
You really know how to make a young man angry
Shirley
Can we get through the night without mentioning family?

The people from your church agree
It's not much of a career
Trying the handles of parked cars
Whoops, there goes another year
Whoops, there goes another pint of beer

Here we are in our summer years
Living on ice cream and chocolate kisses
Would the leaves fall from the trees
If I was your old man and you was my missus?

Shirley
Give my greetings to the new brunette

The Marriage

I understand you needing
And wanting is no crime
But I can't help feeling
That you and your mother are just wasting your time

Choosing Saturdays in summer
I dare you to wear white
Love is just a moment of giving
And marriage is when we admit our parents were right

I just don't understand it
What makes our love a sin?
How can it make that difference
If you and I are wearing that bloody, bloody ring?

If I share my bed with you
Must I also share my life?
Love is just a moment of giving
And marriage is when we admit our parents were right

You just don't understand it
This tender trap we're in
Those glossy catalogues of couples
Are cashing in on happiness again and again

So drag me to the altar
And I'll make my sacrifice
Love is just a moment of giving
And marriage is when we admit our parents were right
And marriage is when we admit our parents were right
I say marriage is when we admit our parents were probably right

Ideology

When one voice rules the nation
Just because they're top of the pile
Doesn't mean their vision is the clearest
The voices of the people
Are falling on deaf ears
Our politicians all become careerists
They must declare their interests
But not their company cars
Is there more to a seat in parliament
Then sitting on your arse?
And the best of all this bad bunch
Are shouting to be heard
Above the sound of ideologies clashing

Outside the patient millions
Who put them into power
Expect a little more back for their taxes
Like school books, beds in hospitals
And peace in our bloody time
All they get is old men grinding axes
Who've built their private fortunes
On the things they can rely
The courts, the secret handshake
The Stock Exchange and the old school tie
For God and Queen and Country
All things they justify
Above the sound of ideologies clashing

God bless the civil service
The nation's saving grace
While we expect democracy
They're laughing in our face
And although our cries get louder
Their laughter gets louder still
Above the sound of ideologies clashing

Levi Stubbs' Tears

With the money from her accident
She bought herself a mobile home
So at least she could get some enjoyment out of being alone
No one could say that she was left up on the shelf
'It's you and me against the world kid,' she mumbled to herself

When the world falls apart some things stay in place
Levi Stubbs' tears run down his face

She ran away from home in her mother's best coat
She was married before she was even entitled to vote
And her husband was one of those blokes
The sort who only laughs at his own jokes
The sort a war takes away and when there wasn't a war he left
    anyway

Norman Whitfield and Barratt Strong
Are here to make right everything that's wrong
Holland and Holland and Lamont Dozier too
Are here to make it all OK with you

And one dark night he came home from the sea
And put a hole in her body where no hole should be
It hurt her more to see him walking out the door
And though they stitched her back together
They left her heart in pieces on the floor

When the world falls apart some things stay in place
She takes off the Four Tops tape and puts it back in its case
When the world falls apart some things stay in place
Levi Stubbs' tears . . .

Honey I'm a Big Boy Now

I can see the kitchen light
From the road where I park my bike
But it's dark there as it often is these days
And the gloomy living room
Really needs a dust and broom
But I can't brush your memory away

Her father was an admiral
In someone else's navy
And she had seen the world before I met her
She would wash and cook and clean
And all the other things between
And like a fool I just sat there and let her

Now I can feed and dress and wash myself
And sleep without the light on
Honey, I'm a big boy now
I don't know what she does with all the money that I send her
She's running round the town with the Young Pretender

I haven't touched the garden
Since the day she walked away
From a love affair that bore only bitter fruit
She took everything she wanted
Which is why she left me here
With these pots and pans and my old wedding suit

A letter came one morning
That she would not let me see
And from that day I began to realise
That she would one day break
The home we tried to make
For sinners cannot live in paradise

There Is Power in a Union

There is power in a factory, power in the land
Power in the hand of the worker
But it all amounts to nothing if together we don't stand
There is power in a union

Now the lessons of the past were all learned with workers'
    blood
Mistakes of the bosses we must pay for
From the cities and the farmlands to trenches full of mud
War has always been the bosses' way, sir

The union forever defending our rights
Down with the blackleg, all workers unite
With our brothers and our sisters from many far off lands
There is power in a union

Now I long for the morning that they realise
Brutality and unjust laws cannot defeat us
But who'll defend the workers who cannot organise
When the bosses send their lackeys out to cheat us?

Money speaks for money, the Devil for his own
Who comes to speak for the skin and the bone?
What a comfort to the widow, a light to the child
There is power in a union

The union forever defending our rights
Down with the blackleg, all workers unite
With our brothers and our sisters together we will stand
There is power in a union

Help Save the Youth of America

Help save the youth of America
Help save them from themselves
Help save the suntanned surfer boys
And their Californian girls

When the lights go out in the rest of the world
What do our cousins say?
They're playing in the sun and having fun, fun, fun
Till Daddy takes the gun away

From the big church to the big river
And out to the shining sea
This is the land of opportunity
And there's a monkey trial on TV

A nation with their freezers full
Is dancing in their seats
While outside another nation
Is sleeping in the streets

Don't tell me the old, old story
Tell me the truth this time
Is the man in the mask or the Indian
An enemy or a friend of mine?

Help save the youth of America
Help save the youth of the world
Help save the boys in uniform
Their mothers and their faithful girls

Listen to the voice of the soldier
Down in the killing zone
Talking about the cost of living
And the price of bringing him home

They're already shipping the body bags
Down below the Rio Grande
But you can fight for democracy at home
And not in some foreign land

And the fate of the great United States
Is entwined in the fate of us all
And the incident at Chernobyl proves
The world we live in is very small

And the cities of Europe have burned before
And they may yet burn again
And if they do I hope you understand
That Washington will burn with them
Omaha will burn with them
Los Alamos will burn with them

Wishing the Days Away

On Monday I wished that it was Tuesday night
So I could wish for the weekend to come
On Tuesday I wished that the night would pass
So I could call you on the phone

Now a man can spend a lot of time
Wondering what was on Jack Ruby's mind
And time is all I have without you here

On Wednesday when you hung up
It was as much as I could do
To stop from wishing Thursday
Would pass so quickly too

They're out there making history
In the Lenin Shipyards today
And here I am in the Hammersmith Hotel
Wishing the days away

There's always room for one more soul
Down in the human zoo
Don't want you to come here though
I want to come home to you

Somebody's knocking at the door
It's later than I think
It's time to put on these stinking clothes
And get out there and stink

Friday I wished that there was something more
To be seen in the letters you send
On Saturday I wished it was Sunday
Oh, will this torment ever end?

Sometimes I take a notion
To put a torch to the tools of my trade
Here I am in the Hammersmith Hotel
Wishing the days away
Here I am in the Hammersmith Hotel
Wishing the days away

The Passion

The fear of a daughter runs high
In the mind of a father to be
For something is growing inside
But we don't talk about it, do we?

In the long, empty, passionless night
Many times to herself she has prayed
That the baby will love her much more
Than the big boy who stole her away

And sometimes it takes a grown man a long time to learn
Just what it would take a child a night to learn

It pains her to know that some things will never be right
If the baby is just someone else to take sides in their fight
Harsh words between bride and groom
The distance is greater each day

He smokes alone in the next room
And she knits her life away

A long time ago she saw visions on the stairs
And when she felt dizzy her mother was always there

The home help is no help at all
I have not committed a crime
Angels gaze down from the wall
Is there a God? Is there a next time?

The Warmest Room

A rainy afternoon
Spent in the warmest room
She lay before me and said
Yes it's true that I have seen some naked men
As she made for the door
Leaving me on the floor
I wish I'd done biology
For an urge within me wanted to do it then

And here she comes again
And I'm sitting on my hands
And she sings to me that siren song
Here she comes again and I'm biting my lip
But it won't be long

As brother Barry said
When he married Marion
The wife has three great attributes:
Intelligence, a Swiss army knife and charm
That's not enough sometimes
And she did speak her mind
And told them all that she believed
The only way to disarm is to disarm

I know people whose idea of fun
Is throwing stones in the river in the afternoon sun
Oh let me be as free as them
Don't let her pass this way again

Though you cannot be blamed
But I've become inflamed
With thoughts of lust and thoughts of power
Thoughts of love and the thoughts of Chairman Mao
We have such little time
At your place or mine
I can't wait till we take our blood tests
Oh baby let's take our blood tests now

The Home Front

Father mows the lawn and Mother peels potatoes
Grandma lays the table alone
And adjusts a photograph of the unknown soldier
In this holy of holies, the home
And from the TV an unwatched voice
Suggests the answer is to plant more trees
The scrawl on the wall says, 'What about the workers?'
And the voice of the people says, 'More salt, please'

Mother shakes her head and reads aloud from the newspaper
While Father puts another lock on the door
And reflects upon the violent times that we are living in
While chatting with the wife beater next door
If paradise to you is cheap beer and overtime
Home truths are easily missed
Something that every football fan knows
It only takes five fingers to form a fist

And when it rains here it rains so hard
But never hard enough to wash away the sorrow
I'll trade my love today for a greater love tomorrow
The lonely child looks out and dreams of independence
From this family life sentence

Mother sees but does not read the peeling posters
And can't believe that there's a world to be won
But in the public schools and in the public houses
The Battle of Britain goes on
The constant promise of jam tomorrow
Is the new breed's litany and verse

If it takes another war to fill the churches of England
Then the world the meek inherit, what will it be worth?

Mother fights the tears and Father his sense of outrage
And attempts to justify the sacrifice
To pass their creed down to another generation
'Anything for the quiet life'
In the Land of a Thousand Doses
Where nostalgia is the opium of the age
Our place in history is as
Clock watchers, old timers, window shoppers

Father mows the lawn and Mother peels potatoes
Oh, how does your garden grow?
And where's that photograph of the unknown soldier
In this holy of holies, the home?
Father reads the mail and Mother will read it later
Grandma cries to herself alone
And adjusts a photograph of the unknown soldier . . .

She's Got a New Spell

What is that sound?
Where is it coming from?
All around
What are you running from?
Something you don't understand
Something you cannot command

That's how I know
That she's got a new spell

What's going down?
Who's moved this room from round me?
Where has it gone?
I fear this night will drown me
So I lie awake all night
'Cos I can't sleep with something I can't fight

The laws of gravity are very, very strict
And you're just bending them for your own benefit

One minute she says
She's gone to get the cat in
The next thing I know
She's mumbling in Latin
She cut the stars out of the sky
And baked them in a pie

She stole the scene and scenery
The script and the machinery

Must I Paint You a Picture?

It's bad timing and me
We find a lot of things out this way
And there's you, a little black cloud in a dress
The temptation to take the precious things
We have apart to see how they work
Must be resisted for they never fit together again
If this is rain let it fall on me and drown me
If these are tears let them fall

Must I paint you a picture
About the way that I feel?
You know my love for you is strong, girl
You know my love for you is real

It took a short walk and a talk
To change the rules of engagement
While you searched frantically for reverse
And then claiming
That virtue never tested is no virtue at all
And so I lost my ignorance
And now the bells across the river chime out your name
I look across to them again

All your friends said come down
It will never fly
And on that imperfect day
We threw it all away
Crisis after crisis, with such intensity
This would never happen if we lived by the sea

Most important decisions in life
Are made between two people in bed
I found that out at my expense
And when I see you
You just turn around and walk away like we never met
Oh, we used to be so brave
I dreamt the world stopped turning as we climbed the hill
I dreamt impossible dreams that we were lovers still

Tender Comrade

What will you do when the war is over, tender comrade?
When we lay down our weary guns?
When we return home to our wives and families
And look into the eyes of our sons?
What will you say of the bond we had, tender comrade?

Will you say that we were brave
As the shells fell all around us
Or that we wept and cried for our mothers
And cursed our fathers
For forgetting that all men are brothers?

Will you say that we were heroes
Or that fear of dying among strangers
Tore our innocence and false shame away?
And from that moment on, deep in my heart I knew
That I would only give my life for love

Brothers in arms, in each other's arms
Was the only time that I was not afraid

What will you do when the war is over, tender comrade?
When we cast off these khaki clothes
And go our separate ways?
What will you say of the bond we had, tender comrade?

The Price I Pay

My friend said she could see no way ahead
And I was probably better off without you
She said to face up to the fact that you weren't coming back
And she could make me happy like you used to
But I'm sorry to say I turned her away
Knowing everything she said was true
And that's the price I pay for loving you the way that I do

There's something inside that hurts my foolish pride
To visit the places we used to go together
Not a day goes by that I don't sit and wonder why
Your feelings for me didn't last forever
Girl I love you so much that sometimes it's such
I'd walk a mile with a stone in my shoe
And that's the price I pay for loving you the way that I do

So keep that phone out of my way for the things I must say
Are empty if you don't believe they're true
That's the price I pay for loving you the way that I do

Girl, I love you so much that baby it's such
I'd walk a mile with a stone in my shoe
And that's the price I pay for loving you the way that I do

Little Time Bomb

One of them's off her food
And the other one's off his head
And both of them are off down the boozer
To drink a toast
To the one that he hates most
And she says there are no winners, only losers

Well if there are no winners
Then what is this he thinks
As he watches her complete a lap of honour
And he sits in the stands
With his head in his hands
And he thinks of all the things
He'd like to bring down upon her

And revenge will bring cold comfort in this darkest hour
As the jukebox says 'It's All Over Now'
And he stands and he screams 'What have I done wrong?
I've fallen in love with a little time bomb'

In public he's such a man
He's punching at the walls with his bare and bloody hands
He's screaming and shouting and acting crazy
But at home he sits alone and he cries like a baby

Oh, he holds your letters but he can't read them
As he fights this loneliness that you call freedom
You said this would happen and you were not wrong
I've fallen in love with a little time bomb

Valentine's Day Is Over

Someday boy you'll reap what you've sown
You'll catch a cold and you'll be on your own
And you will see that what's wrong with me
Is wrong with everyone that
You want to play your little games on

Poetry and flowers, pretty words and threats
You've gone to the dogs again and I'm not placing bets
On you coming home tonight anything but blind
If you take me for granted then you must expect to find
Surprise, surprise

Valentine's Day is over, it's over
Valentine's Day is over

If you want to talk about it, well you know where the phone is
Don't come round reminding me again how brittle bone is

God didn't make you an angel, the Devil made you a man
That brutality and the economy are related now I understand
When will you realise that as above so below there is no love

For the girl with the hour glass figure time runs out very fast
We used to want the same things but that's all in the past
And lately it seems that as it all gets tougher
Your idea of justice just becomes rougher and rougher

Thank you for the things you bought me, thank you for the card
Thank you for the things you taught me when you hit me hard
That love between two people must be based on understanding
Until that's true you'll find your things
All stacked out on the landing
Surprise, surprise

The Only One

Sometimes when you lose your way to me
I think you don't care at all
If you don't get here soon
I'll tear that clock down from the wall

Your family and friends don't understand
They treat me so strange
The book you said to read
Well, I have read but nothing's changed

The clocks go forward, the clocks go back
Yet here I sit as if I were the only one
And oh, you cannot hear me, oh, you cannot hear me
Can anybody hear me out there?

He's up on his high horse again
You're down in the park
I'm left to fight my impulses
Alone here in the dark

The chain that fell off my bike last night
Is now wrapped round my heart
Sometimes I think that
Fate has been against us from the start

I long to let our love run free
Yet here I am, a victim of geography
And oh, you cannot hear me, oh, you cannot hear me
Can anybody hear me out there?

She said, 'Kiss me, or would you rather
Live in a land where the soap won't lather?'
And oh, you know you are the only one
Yes, you are the only one, yes, you are the only one

The Short Answer

Between Marx and marzipan in the dictionary
There was Mary
Between the deep blue sea and the Devil,
That was me
If ever anyone could help me with my obsession with
The young Susannah York
It was Mary

In my pink pyjamas she asked me for something
I gave her the short answer
She read our stars out loud
And I knew then that we should have gone sailing
But we stayed home instead
Fighting on the waterbed like the honeymoon couple on drugs
Me and Mary

What happened in the past
Remained a mystery of natural history
She should have been the last
But she was just the latest
If she wanted to be a farmer's wife
I would endure that muddy life
I would dig for victory

And the sound of happy couples
Coupling happily in the dark
While you and I sat down to tea
I remember you said to me

That no amount of poetry
Would mend this broken heart
But you can put the Hoover round
If you want to make a start

All my friends from school
Introduce me to their spouses
While I'm left standing here
With my hands down the front of my trousers
I just don't know what's to be done
I wonder sometimes, 'How did Dad meet Mum and how did
    they conceive of me?
Tell me, Mary'

The boys who came to the shop
Always made her laugh much more than I did
When I told her this must stop
She didn't bat an eyelid
She said, 'You know honey, it's such a shame
You'll never be any good at this game, you bruise too easily'
So said Mary

Her two brothers took me out
Of circulation for the duration
So we went our separate ways, but does she still love me?
She still has my door key
Like a bully boy in a Benetton shop
You're never happy with what you've got till what you've got
    has gone
Sorry, Mary

Waiting for the Great Leap Forwards

It may have been Camelot for Jack and Jacqueline
But on the Che Guevara highway filling up with gasoline
Fidel Castro's brother spies a rich lady who's crying
Over luxury's disappointment, so he walks over and he's trying
To sympathise with her but he thinks that he should warn her
That the Third World is just around the corner

In the Soviet Union a scientist is blinded
By the resumption of nuclear testing and he is reminded
That Dr Robert Oppenheimer's optimism fell
At the first hurdle

In the Cheese Pavilion and the only noise I hear
Is the sound of someone stacking chairs and mopping up spilt
    beer
And someone asking questions and basking in the light
Of the fifteen fame-filled minutes of the fanzine writer

Mixing pop and politics he asks me what the use is
I offer him embarrassment and my usual excuses
While looking down the corridor
Out to where the van is waiting
I'm looking for the great leap forwards

Jumble sales are organised and pamphlets have been posted
Even after closing time there's still parties to be hosted
You can be active with the activists
Or sleep in with the sleepers
While you're waiting for the great leap forwards

Oh, one leap forward, two leaps back
Will politics get me the sack?
Waiting for the great leap forwards

Well here comes the future and you can't run from it
If you've got a blacklist I want to be on it
Waiting for the great leap forwards

It's a mighty long way down rock'n'roll
From *Top of the Pops* to drawing the dole
You're waiting for the great leap forwards

If no one out there understands
Start your own revolution and cut out the middle man
Waiting for the great leap forwards

In a perfect world we'd all sing in tune
But this is reality so give me some room
Waiting for the great leap forwards

So join the struggle while you may
The revolution is just a T-shirt away
Waiting for the great leap forwards

The Internationale

Stand up, all victims of oppression
For the tyrants fear your might
Don't cling so hard to your possessions
For you have nothing, if you have no rights
Let racist ignorance be ended
For respect makes the empires fall
Freedom is merely privilege extended
Unless enjoyed by one and all

So come brothers and sisters
For the struggle carries on
The Internationale
Unites the world in song
So comrades come rally
For this is the time and place
The international ideal
Unites the human race

Let no one build walls to divide us
Walls of hatred nor walls of stone
Come greet the dawn and stand beside us
We'll live together or we'll die alone
In our world poisoned by exploitation
Those who have taken, now they must give
And end the vanity of nations
We've but one earth on which to live

And so begins the final drama
In the streets and in the fields
We stand unbowed before their armour
We defy their guns and shields

When we fight, provoked by their aggression
Let us be inspired by life and love
For though they offer us concessions
Change will not come from above

I Dreamed I Saw Phil Ochs Last Night

I dreamed I saw Phil Ochs last night
Alive as you and me
Says I to Phil, 'You're ten years dead'
'I never died.' says he
'I never died.' says he

The music business killed you, Phil
They ignored the things you said
And cast you out when fashions changed
Says Phil. 'But I ain't dead'
Says Phil. 'But I ain't dead'

The FBI harassed you, Phil
They smeared you with their lies
Says he. 'But they could never kill
What they could not compromise
I never compromised'

'Though fashion's changed and critics sneered
The songs that I have sung
Are just as true tonight as then
The struggle carries on
The struggle carries on'

When the song of freedom rings out loud
From valleys and from hills
Where people stand up for their rights
Phil Ochs is with us still
Phil Ochs inspires us still

Accident Waiting to Happen

I've always been impressed with a girl
Who could sing for her supper and get breakfast as well
That's the way I am, heaven help me
He said, 'We don't like peace campaigners round here'
As he nailed another one to the wall
And that's what gets me in trouble, heaven help me

Goodbye and good luck to all the promises you've broken
Goodbye and good luck to all the rubbish that you've spoken
Your life has lost its dignity, its beauty and its passion
You're an accident waiting to happen

There you are standing in the bar
And you're giving me grief about the DDR
And that chip on your shoulder gets bigger as you get older
One of these nights you're gonna get caught
It'll give you a pregnant pause for thought
You're a dedicated swallower of fascism

Time up and time out for all the liberties you've taken
Time up and time out for all the friends that you've forsaken
And if you choose to waste away like death is back in fashion
You're an accident waiting to happen

And my sins are so unoriginal
I have all the self-loathing of a wolf in sheep's clothing
In this carnival of carnivores, heaven help me

Moving the Goalposts

I put on my raincoat to make it rain
And sure enough the skies opened up again
I dreamed of you as I walked to the shops
You were dancing with the wallies on *Top of the Pops*

Once in a while
Gennadi Gerasimov drops his smile
And you can see that his aim's
A portfolio pregnant with gains

He's been up all night
Moving the goalposts

Like a jackdaw with a fiery brand
Spread the news all over this land
Robin Hood and his Merry Men
Are never, never, never coming back again

I don't believe that love should be pain
So would you please rub my back again
I think it's safe to leave them in the park
Let's blow out the candles and kiss in the dark

Heavens above
Can this sticky stuff really be love?
Don't get dressed yet
Not yet

We've been up all night
Moving the goalposts

Cindy of a Thousand Lives

Blue Velvet America
Half glimpsed in the headlights between the trees
Who punctured the beauty
And invited monsters such as these?
The pig-faced boy, the corrupted clown
The grotesque figure who never comes into town

Something broken, something stained
Something waiting for the worms to claim
And you can never go there again
Except in nightmares
The voyeur who dares not come near
Knows excitement is merely the beginning of fear

My shadow came this morning
And left some candy in my shoe
They're always watching me
Watching the things I do
Cindy of a thousand lives
Cindy of *The Stepford Wives*

I've looked at all the photographs
But Cindy – which one of them is you?

You Woke Up My Neighbourhood

As I wait for sleep to drag me under
In the evening gloom I sit and wonder
The words I should have said to you
The things I always meant to do
The bad dreams that all came true

You woke up my neighbourhood
Night after night we would row
You woke up my neighbourhood
Things are pretty quiet round here now

When I think of how we were together
I know we couldn't be like that for ever
Beneath the Seven Sisters stars
The night we let it go too far
I slept out in the car

I remember skipping on the porch till it grew cold
I remember feeling like I was eight years old

Somersaults across the lawn
Singing dancing up till dawn
Every now and then we'd have a row
You woke up my neighbourhood
Things are pretty quiet round here now

Trust

He's already been inside me
And he really didn't say
And I really didn't ask him
I just hoped and prayed

He's already been inside me
And I really don't feel well
I keep looking in the mirror
But it's hard to tell

Will he stay by me and take my hand
And hold me till I sleep
Or will he crumble and fall to the floor
And weep
Oh feeble man, oh evil man

He's already been inside me
Would he have told me if he cared?
I know I ought to find out
But I'm much too scared

He's already been inside me
And I know it can't be good
Nothing feels
The way it should

Will he hold me in his arms again
And wipe away my tears
Or has he already taken
My best years
Oh evil man, oh feeble man

God's Footballer

God's footballer hears the voices of angels
Above the choir at Molineux
God's footballer stands on the doorstep
And brings the Good News of the Kingdom to come
While the crowd sings 'Rock of Ages'
The goals bring weekly wages
Yet the glory of the sports pages
Is but the worship of false idols and tempts him not

God's footballer turns on a sixpence
And brings the great crowd to their feet in praise of him
God's footballer quotes from the Gospels
While knocking on doors in the Black Country back streets
He scores goals on a Saturday
And saves souls on a Sunday
For the Lord says these are the Last Days
Prepare thyself for the Judgement yet to come

His career will be over soon
And the rituals of a Saturday afternoon
Bid him a reluctant farewell
For he knows beyond the sport lies the spiritual

The Few

At night the Baby Brotherhood and the Inter-City Crew
Fill their pockets up with calling cards
And paint their faces red, white and blue
And then they go out seeking different-coloured faces
And anyone else that they can scare
And they salute the foes their fathers fought
By waving their right arms in the air
Oh look out, my country's patriots are hunting down below
What do they know of England who only England know?

From the stands of the Empire Stadium
Come the heralds of the new dark age
With the simplicities of bigotry
And to whom all the world's a stage
These little John Bullshits know that the press
Will glorify their feats
So that the general public fear them
And the authorities say give 'em all seats
And the wasted seed of the bulldog breed
Is chanting, 'Here we go'
What do they know of England who only England know?

Our neighbours shake their heads
And take their valuables inside
While my countrymen piss in their fountains
To express our national pride
And to prove to the world that England
Is not as rotten as she looks
They repeat the lies that caught their eyes
At school in history books

But the wars they think they're fighting
Were all over long ago
What do they know of England who only England know?

And the society that spawned them
Just cries out, 'Who's to blame?'
And then wraps itself in the Union Jack
And just carries on the same
Oh look out, my country's patriots are hunting down below
What do they know of England?
What do they know of England?
What do they know of England who only England know?

Sexuality

I've had relations with girls from many nations
I've made passes at women of all classes
And just because you're gay I won't turn you away
If you stick around I'm sure that we can find some common
      ground

Sexuality – strong and warm and wild and free
Sexuality – your laws do not apply to me

A nuclear submarine sinks off the coast of Sweden
Headlines give me headaches when I read them
I had an uncle who once played for Red Star Belgrade
He said that some things are really left best unspoken
But I prefer it all to be out in the open

Sexuality – strong and warm and wild and free
Sexuality – your laws do not apply to me
Sexuality – don't threaten me with misery
Sexuality – I demand equality

I'm sure that everybody knows how much my body hates me
It lets me down most every time and makes me rash and hasty
I feel a total jerk before your naked body of work

I'm getting weighed down with all this information
Safe sex doesn't mean no sex, it just means use your
      imagination
Stop playing with yourselves in hard currency hotels
I look like Robert De Niro, I drive a Mitsubishi Zero

Sexuality – strong and warm and wild and free
Sexuality – your laws do not apply to me
Sexuality – come eat and drink and sleep with me
Sexuality – we can be what we want to be

Tank Park Salute

Kiss me goodnight and say my prayers
Leave the light on at the top of the stairs
Tell me the names of the stars up in the sky
A tree taps on the window pane
That feeling smothers me again
Daddy is it true that we all have to die?
At the top of the stairs
Is darkness

I closed my eyes and when I looked
Your name was in the memorial book
And what had become of all the things we planned?
I accepted the commiserations
Of all your friends and your relations
But there's some things I still don't understand
You were so tall
How could you fall?

Some photographs of a summer's day
A little boy's lifetime away
Is all I've left of everything we've done
Like a pale moon in a sunny sky
Death gazes down as I pass by
To remind me that I'm but my father's son
I offer up to you
This tribute
I offer up to you
This tank park salute

Rumours of War

There are soldiers marching on the common today
They were there again this evening
They paced up and down like sea birds on the ground
Before the storm clouds gathering

I must buy whatever tinned food is left on the shelves
They are testing the air raid sirens
They've filled up the blood banks and emptied the beds
At the hospital and the asylum

I saw a man build a shelter in his garden today
As we stood there idly chatting
He said, 'No, no I don't think war will come'
Yet still he carried on digging

Everything in my life that I love
Could be swept away without warning
Yet the birds still sing and the church bells ring
And the sun came up this morning

Life goes on as it did before
As the country drifts slowly to war

Body of Water

I will cross this body of water
If you promise me you won't try this at home

You're where you want to be
Where am I? I'm up a tree
I had a hurt attack
Rolled away, now I'm bouncing back

Forgive me for feeling sick
I think I just got up too quick
Is this the consequence
Of an out-of-bed experience

Where I'm from the sun don't shine
We keeps the light on all the time
I walk upon the ground you dream about
You finding out about it now
But you are never clever to be found

Summer could take a hint
Seeing you in a floral print
Oh, to become a pearl
In the wordy world of the Cornflake Girl

Don't try this at home
Don't try this at home
Don't try this at home
Don't try this at home

Ontario, Quebec and Me

You don't need my Christmas cards
You already have my heart
This has been a holiday romance
Right from the very start

For we know how to spend the time
Who cares about the weather
We'll dance in the town till the sun goes down
And push our beds together

From the Land of the Midnight Sunglasses
To the mountains of the moon
You could never stay a day too long
Nor never come back too soon

You know what a fool I am
With my short attention span
Flying in the rainy season too
Nothing can keep me away from you

Sulk

If you hate me, why don't you go?
And if you love me, why don't you let me know?
But you just won't give me an inch, so
You just sulk

Why do I want to hide whenever you show up?
You know your moods just make me want to throw up
Why don't you just bloody well grow up?
You just sulk

All of the time
Why don't you pick me up or throw me a line?
All over the place
Why don't you tell me what you think?
Come on and tell me to my face

If you love me, why don't you show it?
If you hate me, why don't you let me know it?
Why don't you just pick up something and throw it?
You just sulk

If you want to bend my arm
Well you could do it with a little more charm
But you just couldn't bear to do me any harm
So you just sulk

And you tell me that you want to quit
And then you treat me like a piece of shit
And when I ask you, 'What's that got to do with it?'
You just sulk

As Long as You Hold Me

As long as you hold me I'll get by
As long as you need me I will try
Not to die

I don't want the shame
I don't want the blame
I don't want the fame, anymore

If only they'd tell me, tell me why
If I could believe them and their lies

But I don't want their name
I don't want their pain
I won't play their games, anymore

I always look at the last page of the book
How will it end? The suspense robs me
Of lovers and friends

From Red to Blue

Another day dawns grey, it's enough to make me spit
But we go on our way, just putting up with it
And when I try to make my feelings known to you
You sound like you have changed from red to blue

You're a father now, you see things in different ways
For every parent will gain perspective on their wilder days
But that alone does not explain the change I see in you
The way you've drifted off from red to blue

Sometimes I think to myself
'Should I vote red for my class or green for our children?'
But whatever choice I make
I will not forsake

So you bought it all, the best your money could buy
And I watched you sell your soul for their bright shining lie
Where are the principles of the friend I thought I knew?
I guess you let them fade from red to blue

I hate the compromises that life forces us to make
We must all bend a little if we are not to break
But the ideals you've opted out of, I still hold them to be true
I guess they weren't so firmly held by you

Upfield

I'm going upfield, way up on the hillside
I'm going higher than I've ever been before
That's where you'll find me, over the horizon
Wading in the river, reaching for that other shore

I dreamed I saw a tree full of angels, up on Primrose Hill
And I flew with them over the Great Wen till I had seen
    my fill
Of such poverty and misery sure to tear my soul apart
I've got a socialism of the heart, I've got a socialism of
    the heart

The angels asked me how I felt about all I'd seen and heard
That they spoke to me, a pagan, gave me cause to doubt their
    word
But they laughed and said: 'I doesn't matter if you'll help us
    in our art
You've got a socialism of the heart, you've got a socialism of
    the heart'

Their faces shone and they were gone and I was left alone
I walked these ancient empire streets till I came tearful to
    my home
And when I woke next morning, I vowed to play my part
I've got a socialism of the heart, I've got a socialism of
    the heart

Brickbat

I ought to leave enough hot water
For your morning bath, but I'd not thought
I hate to hear you talk that way
But I can't bring myself to say I'm sorry

The past is always knocking incessant
Trying to break through into the present
We have to work to keep it out
And I won't be the first to shout it's over

I used to want to plant bombs at the Last Night of the Proms
But now you'll find me with the baby, in the bathroom,
With that big shell, listening for the sound of the sea

I steal a kiss from you in the supermarket
I walk you down the aisle, you fill my basket
And through it all, the stick I take
Is worth it for the love we make

I used to want to plant bombs at the Last Night of the Proms
But now you'll find me with the baby, in the bathroom,
With that big shell, listening for the sound of the sea,
The baby and me

I stayed in bed, alone, uncertain
Then I met you, you drew the curtains
The sun came up, the trees began to sing
And light shone in on everything
I love you

The Space Race Is Over

When I was young I told my mum
I'll walk on the moon someday
Armstrong and Aldrin spoke to me
From Houston and Cape Kennedy
And I watched the Eagle landing
On a night when the moon was full
And as it tugged at the tides, I knew that deep inside
I too could feel its pull

I lay in my bed and dreamed I walked
On the Sea of Tranquillity
I knew that someday soon we'd all sail to the moon
On the high tide of technology
But the dreams had all been taken
And the window seats taken too
And 2001 has almost come and gone
What am I supposed to do?

Now that the space race is over
It's been and it's gone and I'll never get to the moon
Now that the space race is over
And I can't help but feel we've all grown up too soon

Now my dreams have all been shattered
And my wings are tattered too
And I can still fly but not half as high
As once I wanted to

My son and I stand beneath the great night sky
And gaze up in wonder
I tell him the tale of Apollo, and he says
'Why did they ever go?'
It may look like some empty gesture
To go all that way just to come back
But don't offer me a place out in cyberspace
'Cos where in the hell's that at?

Now that the space race is over
It's been and it's gone and I'll never get out of my room
Now that the space race is over
And I can't help but feel we're all just going nowhere

The Fourteenth of February

I wish that I could remember the first moment that we met
If only I could remember that sweet moment that we met
If I knew then that I would spend the rest of my life with you
I imagine I would've held your gaze a little longer when first our
    eyes met

Did it rain or did sunshine attend our first meeting?
What words were said? What weight given to that first greeting?
My diary doesn't help, I don't even mention your name until
    that summer
When bloomed the seed sown on the first day that we met

I know the date, I know the place where it happened
Yet in my mind the scene I recall is imagined
As we grow old I'm sure there will be moments that we will not
    forget
But I would remember something of the moment that we met

King James Version

He was trapped in a haircut he no longer believed in
She said, 'I'm a teacher here. I teach the children'
And he wondered to himself there and then all the things
    he could learn from her
A great mighty wonder

Think of the names you once called me in anger
Remember the sadness in Florence Ballard's eyes
Imagine all the melancholy you could find in the arms of
    a stranger
Bread, bread of heaven

Seems like nothing goes right
In the world that we were born in
But the horizon is bright
Yonder comes the morning

Upstairs they're buying a stairway to Heaven
Down in the Garden they're changing sticks into snakes
And the jangle of religious medals would put the fear of God
    into an angel
Come, come all ye faithful

Their baby came home to them an unmarried mother
They wished she would turn into a pillar of salt
But in the end compassion has to be the greatest family value
Hope, hope of the helpless

Looks like a drift to the right
For the world we were born in
But the horizon is bright
Yonder comes the morning

The Boy Done Good

Strange as it may seem, I once had my football dreams
But I was always the last one, the last to get chosen
When my classmates picked their teams

I guess that was the way it stayed in every game I played
Life just kicked me and clattered and tripped me
Till you picked me from the parade

Now I feel like I've won the cup
Every time that we make love
Forty-five minutes each way
At half-time I hear a brass band play

The boy done good, the girl done better
The seasons turn and we're still together
The sky's still blue and tomorrow is another day

You weren't that kind of a bird
Who likes her studs to be covered in mud
Taking you to the pictures was a regular fixture
For one of life's eternal subs

Though I tried hard acting tough
I just can't stand the taste of that stuff
Like some macho park player I got in the way of
In some grudge match against his club

Still I'm happier where I am today
Now I've put my boots away
I guess I'll never get picked to play
My song on *Match of the Day*

St Monday

Monday and the afternoon is bearing down on me
I'm watching the clock and the clock is watching me
Don't have to be cool but you know I am
Don't have to be here but you know that

I'm a hard worker but I ain't working on a Monday
I'm a hard worker but I ain't working on a Monday
A hard-working fellow but I ain't working on a Monday
St Monday's still the weekend to me

Two dozen enquiries are on hold for me
My shift supervisor is staring hard at me
Nobody can say what the matter is
I'm trying to recharge my batteries

Somewhere out on the road, I just wanna be free
I don't wanna do as I'm told
Don't wanna work four, five, six days and turnaround
Want to get high on life but first I got to get me back home

Nobody can say what the matter is
I'm trying to recharge my batteries

England, Half English

My mother was half English
And I'm half English too
I'm a great big bundle of culture
Tied up in the red, white and blue
I'm a fine example of your Essex Man
And I'm well familiar with the Hindustan
'Cos my neighbours are half English
And I'm half English too

My breakfast was half English
And so am I you know
I had a plate of Marmite soldiers
Washed down with a cappuccino
And I have a veggie curry about once a week
The next day I fry it up as bubble'n'squeak
'Cos my appetite's half English
And I'm half English too

Dance with me
To this very English melody
From Morris dancing to Morrissey
All that stuff came from across the sea

Britannia , she's half English
She speaks Latin at home
St George was born in the Lebanon
How he got here I don't know
And those three lions on your shirt
They never sprang from England's dirt
Them lions are half English
And I'm half English too

Le-li Umma le-li-ya, le-li Umma le-li-ya
Le-li Umma le-li-ya, bledi g'desh akh! le-li-ya
Oh my country, oh my country
Oh my country, what a beautiful country you are

NPWA

I grew up in a company town
And I worked real hard
Till that company closed down
They gave my job to another man
On half my wages in some foreign land
But when I asked
How could this be any good for our economy
I was told nobody cares
So long as they make money
When they sell their shares

Can you hear us?
Are you listening?
No power without accountability
Are you listening?
No power without accountability

I lost my job, my car and my house
When 10,000 miles away some guy clicked on a mouse
He didn't know me, we never spoke
He didn't ask my opinion
Or canvass for my vote
I guess it's true, nobody cares
Till those petrol bombs
Come spinning through the air
Gotta find a way to hold them to account
Before they find a way to snuff our voices out

The ballot box is no guarantee
That we achieve democracy
Our leaders claim their victory
When only half the people have spoken
We have no job security
In this global economy
Our borders closed to refugees
But our markets forced open

The World Bank says to Mexico
'We'll cut you off if you don't keep your taxes low'
But they have no right to wield that sword
'Cos they take their orders
From the chairman of the board

IMF, WTO
I hear these words just every place I go
Who are these people?
Who elected them?
And how do I replace them with some of my friends?

Take Down the Union Jack

Take down the Union Jack, it clashes with the sunset
And put it in the attic with the Emperor's old clothes
When did it fall apart? Sometime in the '80s
When the great and the good gave way to the greedy and
    the mean

Britain isn't cool you know
And it's really not that great
It's not a proper country
It doesn't even have a patron saint
It's just an economic union
That's past its sell-by date

Take down the Union Jack, it clashes with the sunset
And ask our Scottish neighbours if independence looks any
    good
'Cos they just might understand how to take an abstract
    notion
Of personal identity and turn it into nationhood

Is this the nineteenth century
That I'm watching on TV?
The dear old Queen of England
Handing out those MBEs
Member of the British Empire
That doesn't sound too good to me

Gilbert and George
Are taking the piss, aren't they?
Gilbert and George are taking the piss
What could be more British than
'Here's a picture of me bum'?
Gilbert and George are taking the piss

Take down the Union Jack, it clashes with the sunset
And pile up all those history books but don't throw them away
'Cos they just might have a clue about what it really means
To be an Anglo hyphen Saxon in England dot co dot UK

Tears of My Tracks

I'm down but I'm not out
But Lord I'm hurting
I'm down but I'm not out
But I feel blue

I sold all my vinyl yesterday
At a boot sale out on the highway
And now my room is full of fresh air

Somebody owns all my albums now
They probably don't even wonder how
My name got written on the sleeves

I opened the window, I let in the sun
My record collection has ended
For someone else it's just begun

Yarra Song

There's a chill tonight on the Yarra
Winter is creeping in
While far away my loved ones
Wake up in England's spring

And although delights await me
All the way to Flinders Street
It's that little piece of heaven
With which they must compete

When The Saints take on The Magpies
Someday too far away
I barrack for St Kilda
In that funny game they play

But my heart's not really in it
My mind wanders to a town
Where the Hammers sing 'I'm Forever Blowing Bubbles'
And the rain comes pouring down

Yes, it's still raining in England
Guess that's why I like it here
There's a brolly in my hotel room
For when the skies aren't clear

'Cos it never rains in Sydney
And it never rains in Perth
Adelaide's a desert
And Brisbane's just scorched earth

So excuse me please such days as there
And send me to the town
Where the children sing when St Kilda win
And the rain comes falling down

So wake me up tomorrow
And send me home again
To where the Hammers sing 'I'm Forever Blowing Bubbles'
In the pouring London rain

Old Clash Fan Fight Song

I've got a mate who lives in Vermont
He couldn't find the music he wants
Sick and tired of the corporations
Started his own little radio station
Now he's on the air each day
Telling folks about a different way
He plays Billy Bragg and a bit of Green Day
And 'I'm So Bored with the USA'

People are on the move
People got a lot to prove

I've got a buddy who delivers the post
Up and down the northeast coast
When The Clash came to town
He never missed 'em
He still wants to bust the system
But he has to go to work
That doesn't mean he's some kind of a jerk
He puts food on the table
You know how that feels?
It doesn't mean he's lost his ideals

People are moving on
George Bush will soon be gone

The clampdown is still coming down hard
Police and thieves all over my yard
But these heavy manners don't worry me
'Cos I'm a heavier dude than I used to be

People are moving on
Tony Blair will soon be gone

Cooperation – not competition
Cooperation is not sedition

I Keep Faith

If you want to make the weather
Then you have to take the blame
If sometimes dark clouds fill the sky
And it starts to rain and folks complain
And though your head may tell you
To run and hide
Listen to your heart and you'll find me
Right by your side

Because I keep faith
I keep faith
I keep faith
I keep faith in you

If you think you have the answer
Well don't be surprised
If what you say is met with anger
And contempt and lies
No matter how hard you may want to
Just walk away
Reach out you'll find me there beside you
All of the way
Because I keep faith
I keep faith in you

All the dreams we shared
I never knew no one who cared
About these things the way that I've seen you
It doesn't matter if
This all falls off the cliff
Together we are gonna see it through

I know it takes a mess of courage
To go against the grain
You have to make great sacrifice for such little gain
And so much pain
And if your plans have come to nothing
Washed out in the rain
Let me rekindle all your hopes
And help you start again

M for Me

Take the M for me and the Y for you
Out of family and it all falls through
We've got to love each other every day
Instead of hoping it might stay that way

I've got friends who are telling me
They're living in clover
But lose the C for commitment and the L for love
And it's over baby, it's all over now

I'm not thinking about the things you said
As we lay awake last night in bed
I'm just happy to be by your side
When we're rolling in the sheets or tumbling in the tide

You keep on come telling me all about your problems
Let's pull the Y off of your and throw it on the fire
And make 'em our problems baby
Our problems now

Take the M for me and the Y for you
Out of family and it all falls through
We've got to love each other every day
Instead of hoping it might stay that way

Your problems baby
Make 'em our problems now

Something Happened

Do you know what love is?
Love is when you willingly
Place someone else's priorities
Above your own

Do you know what lust is?
Lust is when you actively
Force your own priorities
On someone else

January Song

I'm so tightly wound in tension
Feel just like a guitar string
Waiting to reveal emotions
Touch me and you'll hear me sing

I'm so tired of being wired
But there's so much I have to do
Tidy up the place for Monday
When she's buried in her dancing shoes

My journey has been so hard lately
Been having to get out and push
Left me standing on the sidewalk
Talking to a burning bush

Politician selling freedom
Bumper sticker 50 cents
Ask him what he wants to be free from
Answer don't make any sense

Somewhere on the far horizon
Going to wash away my sins
Turn around and taste tomorrow
This is how the end begins

Handyman Blues

I'm never going to be the handyman
Around the house my father was
So don't be asking me to hang
A curtain rail for you because

That screwdriver business just gets me confused
It takes me half an hour to change a fuse
And when I flicked the switch the lights all blew
I'm not your handyman

Don't be expecting me to put up shelves
Or build a garden shed
But I can write a song that tells the world
How much I love you instead

I'm not any good at pottery
So let's lose a 't' and just shift back the 'e'
And I'll find a way to make my poetry
Build a roof over our heads

I know it looks like I'm just reading the paper
But these ideas I'll turn to gold dust later
'Cos I'm a writer, not a decorator
I'm not your handyman

Do unto Others

In the Bible we are told
God gave Moses in the days of old
Ten great commandments
For his people to hold true
But the greatest commandment of all
Is in the Book of Luke as I recall:
Do unto others as you would have them do to you

It may be you don't believe
In the story of Adam and Eve
And call upon science
To prove it's all untrue
But in the cold light of the day
These simple words still point the way
Do unto others as you would have them do to you

So just lift up your eyes
Don't pass by on the other side
Don't be bound by what you think others may do
A little bit of faith
That's all it really takes
Do unto others as you would have them do to you

Now the way the world is run
Too many people looking after number one
Don't seem to notice
The damage that they do
Though it's not widely understood
There is a greater good
Do unto others as you would have them do to you

Goodbye, Goodbye

Goodbye to all my friends
The time has come for me to go
Goodbye to all the souls
Who sailed with me so long

The day has come at last
The sails strain at the mast
The years have quickly passed away

The bells have all been rung,
The songs have all been sung,
This long river has run its course

The coffee pot is cold,
The jokes have all been told,
The last stone has been rolled away

Goodbye to all my friends
The time has come for me to say
Goodbye to all the souls
Who've sailed with me along the way

Goodbye, goodbye

Tomorrow's Going to Be a Better Day

To the misanthropic, misbegotten merchants of gloom
Who look into their crystal balls and prophesise our doom
Let the death knell chime, it's the end of time
Let the cynics put their blinkers on and toast our decline

Don't become demoralised by this chorus of complaint
It's a sure sign that the old world is terminally quaint

Tomorrow's going to be a better day
No matter what the siren voices say
Tomorrow's going to be a better day
We're going to make it that way

To the pessimistic populists who harbour no doubt
That every day we make our way to Hell in a handcart
And the snarky set who are sniping to get
Anyone who sticks their head above the parapet

Don't be disheartened baby, don't be fooled,
Take it from someone who knows: the glass is half full

Tomorrow's going to be a better day
No matter what the siren voices say
Tomorrow's going to be a better day
We're going to make it that way

Song of the Iceberg

Once I was a dewdrop
A million years ago
Rose up on a misty day
Into the clouds and rolled away

Reborn as a raindrop
I fell to earth as rain
To rise and fall and rise and fall
And rise and fall again

Rise and fall, freshwater and brine
Rise and fall and rise and fall until the end of time
Rise and fall, freshwater and brine
Rise and fall and rise and fall until the end of time

Once I was a snowflake
Ten thousand years ago
Drifting in a blizzard deep
Fell into a frozen sleep

Reborn as an iceberg
We calved in Baffin Bay
And waited for the moon-hauled tides
To carry us away

A single fleeting moment
In a vast ocean of time
Floating on a night so calm
Pass me by, I mean no harm

A mountain made of raindrops
Goes drifting on its way
And dreams of making rainbows
On some distant summer's day

Notes

COSMONAUT

'Cosmonaut' marked a watershed in my songwriting, the moment when I stopped using the music of the 1960s as my inspiration and began to write songs in a contemporary style. In early 1977, I saw the Clash for the first time and realised that there was something really exciting happening right here and right now in my city. I cut my hair short, swapped my flares for some drainpipe trousers and began writing songs inspired by the burgeoning punk movement.

My tunes became shorter, chord progressions less standard and, where I had hitherto written lyrics aimed at endearing myself to the listener, I began to compose songs that revelled in their outsider status.

'I Wanna Be A Cosmonaut' was the title track of a four-song extended play record by Riff Raff released on Chiswick Records in June 1978

THE MILKMAN OF HUMAN KINDNESS

When I was growing up, milk was delivered in pint bottles to almost every household in Britain by a milkman. If more was needed, a note would be left in the neck of an empty milk bottle asking for 'an extra pint today please'. The idea that the milk of human kindness – a phrase coined by Shakespeare – could be distributed in the same way gave me a simple metaphorical image on which to hang this song.

Originally entitled 'Love versus the Incredible Sulk', the first version involved a longer list of promises, including, 'If you are busy, I will walk your dog'.

This is the most political song on my first album and, like my attitudes at the time, the politics are personal rather than ideological. Me and my schoolmates had been educated to work at the car factory but in the early 1980s a new type of worker was emerging from the service industries set up to support the booming financial sector. The deregulation that allowed them to get on the gravy train consigned many of those in manufacturing, who had relied on social solidarity to provide them with job security, to the scrapheap.

My reasoned political arguments against these young upwardly mobile professionals weren't yet formulated. Instead, the best I could manage was this visceral response.

RICHARD

I'd gone round to my friend Neil's house to watch Nottingham Forest on their way to winning the 1979 European Cup. His sister Jayne had a new boyfriend named Richard who she insisted on telling us all about, despite the fact that we were trying to watch the match. For some reason, possibly to annoy her for annoying us, I started taking notes. When I got home, I turned these scribbled phrases into this song. At some point in the evening, someone said 'every alpha particle has a helium nucleus' but unfortunately this didn't quite fit the scansion of the melody, so I tweaked it a bit, which you're not really allowed to do in physics. This might explain why I failed my science exams.

Look and Learn was a weekly educational magazine for children that sought to explain the world and all its complexity through the medium of cutaway drawings.

'Richard' was the first song I wrote that I felt was distinctive enough to be considered a Billy Bragg song, and the only Riff Raff song that survived my transition to solo performer.

I utilised other songs that I'd written during the time I was in the band, but this was the only one we'd ever played live.

A NEW ENGLAND

One night, stargazing on the way back from the pub, I saw two tiny spots of light, flying alongside one another, slowly cross the sky. I assumed they were satellites, but the incurable romantic in me saw two star-crossed lovers turned into shooting stars by their passion for one another. I hurried home and wrote this song.

You might ask why this one never made it into the Riff Raff set, given its later popularity. The simple reason is that the very next day I wrote a song called 'The Kitten', which immediately worked as a band number, somewhat overshadowing my previous day's efforts. As a result, 'A New England' was left on the shelf. When I dusted it off for later use, I was reminded of a line from 'The Leaves That Are Green' by Simon and Garfunkel. I had been twenty-one years old when I first composed this song. Now here I was, a year later, rewriting it to fit my changed circumstances. 'Time hurries on,' I thought to myself as I borrowed Paul Simon's words for my opening lines.

The message of the chorus is a simple one: it's exhausting trying to change the world and create a new society. Sometimes you just need someone to hug.

THE MAN IN THE IRON MASK

Taking its title from the writings of French novelist Alexandre Dumas, 'The Man in the Iron Mask' sprang from my attempt to work out the chords to the Sandy Denny song 'Fotheringay', about the execution of Mary Queen of Scots in 1587. I never did work out how to play it, but I uncovered an interesting chord progression, which developed into this song.

I was never a brilliant guitar player, so it was tricky for me to play at first, being almost all barre chords. I persevered with it because it utilised a little musical trick that would later feature in tracks like 'The Saturday Boy' and 'Levi Stubbs' Tears'. It involves dropping the forefinger of the barre chord a semitone on the bottom E string to create a pleasing passing chord. Wiggy taught me how to do it. I think he nicked it off a Faces record.

THE BUSY GIRL BUYS BEAUTY

'The Busy Girl Buys Beauty' was the title of an article in *Woman's Realm*, a weekly magazine that my mother read. 'Top Tips for the Gas Cook', 'The Daily Drill for Beautiful Hair' and 'The Truth About Pain' all came from the same source. 'Successful Secrets of a Sexual Kind' sounds to me like I made it up, but it may have appeared there too.

Anna Ford and Angela Rippon were the first female anchors on ITV and BBC news, respectively, and quickly became style icons for that generation of women.

LOVER'S TOWN REVISITED

'Lover's Town' was a Riff Raff song that spoke of a time when it seemed I couldn't go anywhere without being threatened or beaten up by some gang or other. Joining a band gave me my own gang and saved me from having to put myself in jeopardy in order to socialise. 'Lover's Town Revisited' is also from the Riff Raff period, and was originally titled 'Summer of the Evening'.

IT SAYS HERE

The Times newspaper ran a series of adverts in the early 1980s with the slogan 'Have you ever wished that you were better informed?' One showed Julius Caesar smiling on the steps of the Forum while conspirators crept up behind him, daggers drawn.

When the British newspapers were all printed in and around Fleet Street in London, 'The Street of Shame' was a term used to describe the tabloid end of the market.

THE MYTH OF TRUST

One Saturday in the summer of 1984, I went down to Hammersmith to buy some swimming trunks and, while waiting for the bus home, saw this amazing guitar for sale in a shop window. It was a Burns Steer, possibly the very first one made, and I took it home with me. It came to define my guitar style, perhaps best described as 'chop and clang'. I found it too late into the recording of *Brewing Up* for it to make much of an impression on the overall sound of the album, but the spooky lows of the bass strings and cutting treble of the tops on this cut could only come from the Steer.

FROM A VAUXHALL VELOX

Vauxhall was a British car company that was taken over by General Motors in 1925. In the late 1950s they produced the Velox PA SY, perhaps the most American-style car ever manufactured in the UK. It had tail fins, a three-part rear window and a massive bench seat in the front. When it came time for me to write a car song, there was only one model that would do the trick. The title is paraphrased from a Bob Dylan song.

THE SATURDAY BOY

A Saturday boy, or girl, is a youth of school age who works part time in a shop at the weekend. Between the ages of thirteen and sixteen, I was the Saturday boy at a hardware store called Guy Norris on Station Parade in Barking. I spent my days helping people to choose their wallpaper, weighing out nuts and bolts, and making copious cups of tea for the staff. The great attraction of the job was that the shop also contained a record store in the basement, where, as a member of staff, I got a discount. My weekly wages were invariably spent before I got them home.

When word got out that I worked at Guy Norris, I became popular with the girls in my class as someone who could get them cheap copies of *Hunky Dory*, but not popular enough to be considered as a slow-dance partner at the school disco.

'La La Means I Love You' by the Delfonics spent ten weeks in the UK charts in 1971 and was a popular slow dance at the school disco.

ISLAND OF NO RETURN

The Falklands War of 1982 came just a year after my short spell in the British Army, so it should be no surprise to find that when I chose to write a song about the conflict, it should be from a soldier's perspective.

Salisbury Plain is the site of a huge military training area in southern England.

It was reported during the war that some Argentine troops were equipped with British-made weapons. Birmingham was traditionally the centre of British arms manufacturing.

The Sun newspaper was accused of gross insensitivity when it used the headline 'GOTCHA!' to report of the sinking of the Argentine light cruiser General Belgrano, with the loss of 323 lives.

Three-quarters of the couplet 'Me and the Corporal out on a spree / Damned from here to eternity' is borrowed from the Rudyard Kipling poem 'Gentleman-Rankers'.

ST SWITHIN'S DAY

Swithin (or Swithun) was a ninth-century Anglo-Saxon saint-whose feast day is 15 July. An old proverb holds that, if it rains on St Swithin's Day, it will continue to rain for the following forty days.

The song was originally called 'St Crispin's Day', but for some reason I can't recall, I changed its patron saint. This confusion is reflected in the fourth line of the song. The Battle of Agincourt was fought on St Crispin's Day in 1415.

This is another track that benefited from the arrival of the Burns Steer. Its ringing tones between each verse were the basis for the song, sounding to me like the pealing of church bells.

A LOVER SINGS

Page 9 of the *New Musical Express* dated 24 March 1984 carried a full-page advert for the new single from Prefab Sprout – 'Couldn't Bear to Be Special'. Featuring a portrait of Prefabs front man Paddy McAloon looking pensive, the layout left wide empty margins on either side of the picture. I was travelling on a train when the lyrics to this song began to come to me and, with no notepaper to hand, I jotted them down in the vast open spaces of the advert.

BETWEEN THE WARS

The election of Ronald Reagan in 1981 produced a sudden plunge in temperature of the Cold War. Reagan's belligerent attitude to the Soviet Union, echoed in Europe by British Prime Minister Margaret Thatcher, made the possibility of nuclear conflict seem highly likely. So tangible was this sense of impending doom that when, in October 1983, the ABC network screened a television film about a full-scale nuclear exchange between the United States and the Soviet Union, it was watched by over 100 million people in the US. *The Day After* remains the TV film with the largest audience in history, and is perhaps the most bleak.

In the UK, the government added to the general sense of unease by printing thousands of leaflets to be distributed in the event of nuclear war. Entitled 'Protect and Survive', they offered handy hints about how to build a nuclear shelter in your living room. The Soviet Union played its part too, nervously shooting down a Korean Air Lines flight that it felt had strayed too close to Soviet airspace in September 1983.

It was against this backdrop that I wrote 'Between the Wars'. The terrible sense of drift towards world war, coupled with soaring unemployment and rising union militancy, gave the impression that we were back in the 1930s, and I peppered the lyrics with images from that period.

'From cradle to grave': those who built the welfare state in the post-war years believed that the government should provide all citizens with social security – free health care, free education and decent, affordable housing – 'from the cradle to the grave'.

SCHOLARSHIP IS THE ENEMY OF ROMANCE

You meet this girl and you're immediately attracted to her, not least because she's really clever. You build a relationship, but then she goes off to university and meets new and exciting people. Where does that leave you?

I DON'T NEED THIS PRESSURE, RON

By the time this song was released as the B-side of 'Days Like These' in December 1985, I had spent two years explaining my politics to people and dealing with the expectations that were aroused by my more polemical songs. At the same time I had to defend myself from the spurious idea that, because I sold a lot of records, I was somehow disqualified from talking about inequality. I wrote this as a response and still hold it to be my credo.

The title is a pun on the chorus of Spandau Ballet's 'Chant No. 1'.

GREETINGS TO THE NEW BRUNETTE

An ex-girlfriend – whose name wasn't Shirley – sent me a post-card to tell me that she'd dyed her hair, signing it 'Greetings from the new brunette'. The phrase stuck with me and then attached itself to this song.

The 1984 miners' strike was my political education, intro-ducing me not only to socialism but also to sexual politics. While I found this pretty straightforward on paper, it could prove a little tricky in relationships. I clearly had a lot to learn and this song attempts to chart that process.

'Lie back and think of England' is the Victorian mother's advice to her daughter when asked what to do on her wedding night.

THE MARRIAGE

This dates from a time in my life when I was getting through relationships with the speed and commitment of a flat stone skimming over a lake. Throughout this period, there was one woman who kept banging on about getting married – my mum. This song is directed at her rather than at any specific girlfriend.

IDEOLOGY

The Clash were the band that turned me on to radical politics – their support for Rock Against Racism led me to undertake my first political activism in 1978, marching through the streets of London in opposition to the neo-fascist National Front. Yet I've always felt that their failure to connect with mainstream politics had limited their ability to be a catalyst for change.

However, my belief in parliamentary democracy was severely tested during the Red Wedge campaign. Far from being committed to radical change, elements of the Labour Party were just time-serving hacks who had little interest in engaging with a new generation of potential Labour voters. While they might make a great show of displaying their differences with the Tories in the Commons, underneath the rhetoric, they were much the same.

LEVI STUBBS' TEARS

This tune sprang out of the Burns Steer guitar and I wrote the lyrics on a cross-Channel ferry. Andy Kershaw, who was then my road manager, called his autobiography *No Off Switch*, and he wasn't kidding. In the hope of getting a little peace and quiet, I told him I was writing a song and couldn't chat anymore. I'd had the title running around in my head for a while so I duly wrote it on a piece of paper and, in the middle of the English Channel, these lyrics began to emerge.

Levi Stubbs was the lead singer of the Four Tops, who had numerous hits on the Motown label from the mid-'60s to the early '70s. Most of those songs were provided by the songwriting and production team of Eddie Holland, Brian Holland and Lamont Dozier. Norman Whitfield and Barrett Strong were another team of Motown songwriters, working most successfully with the Temptations.

HONEY I'M A BIG BOY NOW

After I'd spent a couple of weeks opening for the Smiths in the US, Morrissey commented that my act was 'positively vaudevillian'. I don't know if he meant it as a compliment, but I certainly took it as one. The fact that he'd noticed there was a touch of the music hall in what I did pleased me no end, as I've always felt I had as much in common with Max Miller as I do with Mick Jagger.

My grandmother used to play an upright piano at family gatherings and we'd all gather round to sing the old music-hall songs that she loved. It's Kenny Craddock playing here, not my nan, but he does a decent job of capturing the spirit of her enthusiastic style.

THERE IS POWER IN A UNION

During the miners' strike, I shared the bill at many benefits with folk singers who performed songs written by Joe Hill. Born in Sweden in 1879, Hill emigrated to the US around the turn of the century and became active in the Industrial Workers of the World, the 'one big union'. He was their primary songwriter, penning new lyrics to old tunes. One of his songs is called 'There Is Power in a Union'.

While travelling around the country during the year of the strike, I got the notion to write a song in Hill's style, so, borrowing the tune from an American Civil War ballad variously known as 'Rally Round the Flag' or 'The Battle Cry of Freedom', I appropriated Hill's title and wrote some new lyrics. I'm proud to say that my version ended up next to Joe's in the IWW's *Little Red Songbook*.

HELP SAVE THE YOUTH OF AMERICA

This song takes its title from a leaflet produced by the Ku Klux Klan in Louisiana in 1965 that proclaimed 'Help Save the Youth of America – Don't Buy Negro Records'. Offensive though this shocking piece of segregationist propaganda was, it got me thinking that there were other things that the youth of America needed saving from – not least their leader's seeming determination to initiate a thermonuclear war with the Soviet Union.

WISHING THE DAYS AWAY

One of the painful paradoxes of being an itinerant worker is that you develop a longing to be home with those you love. Making my living as a musician was what I'd always wanted to do and I really enjoyed touring the world. But such was the nature of my success in the mid-'80s that I'd only be home for a week or two before I was headed off on tour again. Inevitably, that kind of schedule plays havoc with your relationships.

Jack Ruby was the man who shot Lee Harvey Oswald, and Oswald was the man who shot John F. Kennedy.

The Lenin Shipyards in Gdańsk, Poland, was the birthplace of Solidarity, the first independent trade union in the Soviet bloc.

THE PASSION

Pregnancy, if not planned, can knock the wheels off a love affair, putting all the pressure on the woman, leaving the man bewildered, unschooled. Like so much in relationships, consent is the key to a happy ending.

THE WARMEST ROOM

If you'd have walked in and caught the two of us, there on the floor, discussing naked men, you'd have known right away what was happening.

I put a lot of work into this song, trying to distil the frustrations of being trapped in your parents' world while you're desperate to escape into your own. On the very last day of mixing, I recall lying on the floor of Livingstone Studios trying to finish the lyrics so that I could record the vocal and complete the album. It was long past midnight when we finally added the sample of 'Jerusalem' to the fade out. The next morning I left for back-to-back tours of Japan and East Germany. Happy days.

SHE'S GOT A NEW SPELL

A friend lived next door to a professional witch, who placed a card in the window of the local newsagents offering to cast spells that could make someone fall in love with you. One night we were round his house and heard the faint sound of chanting coming through the walls. 'Sounds like she's got a new spell,' said our host, and I began wondering what it would be like to be the subject of one of her enchantments.

WALK AWAY RENÉE (VERSION)

When Johnny Marr came to visit during the *Taxman* sessions, I invited him to play on 'Greetings to the New Brunette'. While the engineer was setting up mics around him, Johnny began to play a beautiful instrumental version of 'Walk Away Renée' on my Martin D18 acoustic. We liked it so much that we recorded a take and I wrote the monologue as I travelled home that night on the Tube from Wood Green to Chiswick Park.

Fittingly, this became the B-side of 'Levi Stubbs' Tears', the Four Tops having scored a hit with 'Walk Away Renée' in 1968.

MUST I PAINT YOU A PICTURE?

Workers Playtime is my break-up album, mostly written during the collapse of a truly titanic love affair. For once, my songs weren't enough to hold her attention, so maybe painting a picture might help.

I live by the sea now, so this kind of thing never happens.

TENDER COMRADE

You only have to see old soldiers get together to know that the bonds forged in the heat of battle go much deeper than those found in civilian life.

THE PRICE I PAY

The Mint Juleps were a female a capella sextet from East London who supported me on a couple of tours. When they asked me to write them a song, I thought I'd try to come up with something in the style of the great Sam Cooke. For whatever reason, they never got around to recording it, so I cut it instead.

Producer Joe Boyd came up trumps when he invited Danny Thompson, ex-bass player of Pentangle, to join the *Workers Playtime* sessions. Danny, who had backed John Martyn and Tim Buckley, plays with great sensitivity and has a wicked sense of humour. Joe's choice of drummer was not so successful. When he bailed after the first day, Wiggy, who was working with me on the album, suggested we put out a call to Mickey Waller, who had played on the classic Rod Stewart albums that we had worshipped as teenagers.

He duly appeared, and while setting up his drum kit for this number, he and Danny, trying to think where they had met before, came to the conclusion that the last time they'd played together was at the recording of 'Maggie May' – Rod Stewart's biggest hit. Me and Wiggy looked at each other and were teenagers again. We couldn't stop grinning for the rest of the evening.

LITTLE TIME BOMB

You know how it is, things come to a head and you go down to the pub to try to sort it all out amicably and suddenly the whole thing blows up in your face.

VALENTINE'S DAY IS OVER

I once got buttonholed about this song by a trio of feminists who didn't think I should be writing songs from a female perspective. 'You'll never know what it really feels like to be the victim of male violence', they told me, and I had to agree. However, I didn't write this song for women – there are plenty of powerful songs by women that address this issue. I wrote it for men, that they should hear from another man that violence towards women is never acceptable, under any circumstances.

THE ONLY ONE

When I went to Moscow in 1987, they put me up in the Hotel Ukraina, a grandiose slice of high Soviet architecture. My room contained a freestanding bath and every morning I would submerge myself there while listening to *Astral Weeks* and sipping Red Zinger tea made with boiling water from a sturdy bedside samovar. It was my way of easing myself into the strangeness of the Soviet Union.

The one annoying thing about my stay there was that I had trouble getting the soap to lather. I never worked out whether this was down to the hardness of the Moscow water, the cheapness of the hotel soap or because communism was inherently inferior to capitalism.

To maintain the bath-related theme, this song is the sound of a relationship going down the plughole.

Between Marx and marzipan was where I spent much of the 1980s, never feeling totally comfortable at either of these extremes: one was too bitter, the other too sweet a position from which to observe the world. I was always happiest writing songs from a place where a wry sense of humour could be used to shed light on relationships and ideals that never quite delivered on their initial promise.

Susannah York was an English actress who rose to fame in the 1960s.

And Mary, the tall girl, the barefoot girl, the little black cloud in a dress, the only one, the price I paid, the little time bomb – she was, to everybody else's dismay, the object of my doomed affections.

WAITING FOR THE GREAT LEAP FORWARDS

Workers Playtime wasn't only a break-up album, it was also my post-political album. The 1984 miners' strike had given artists the chance to be polemical and I grabbed that opportunity with both hands, doing my best to push the pop and politics agenda, culminating in the Red Wedge initiative supporting the Labour Party at the 1987 general election.

But the miners had lost and Mrs Thatcher had been re-elected on a landslide. The barricades had been overrun and several trips behind the Iron Curtain had tempered my enthusiasm for seeing politics in black and white terms. Most of all, I'd become starkly aware of the limits of trying to change the world by singing songs.

Despite all that, I still believed that music had a role to play in offering a different perspective on things, from the minutiae of relationships to the great geo-political arguments of the day. This song was my way of owning up to the ambiguities of being a political pop star while stating clearly that I still believed in Sam Cooke's promise that a change was gonna come.

Jack Kennedy was the 35th president of the United States, and Jacqueline was his wife. Together they were said to have created a 'Camelot' at the White House between 1960 and 1963.

Robert Oppenheimer is known as the 'Father of the Atom Bomb' for his role in the design and construction of the first of such weapons.

The Cheese Pavilion is a venue near Shepton Mallet in Somerset, where I did a gig in the 1980s. Part of a large agricultural showground, its main purpose is to house regular contests to find the finest cheeses in England.

'It's a mighty long way down rock 'n' roll' is a line from the chorus of 'All the Way from Memphis' by Mott the Hoople, a song about the disconcerting paradoxes of pop stardom.

THE INTERNATIONALE

I was really pleased when the Berlin Wall came down and the communist regimes of Eastern Europe began to melt away. However, I wasn't so happy when Western triumphalism sought to use this as an excuse to tip all aspects of left-wing culture into the trash. The people of Eastern Europe had been liberated from totalitarianism but they had not been freed from exploitation. Songs of solidarity would still be needed by those struggling for a fairer society. Encouraged by Pete Seeger, I undertook the task of updating this most traditional of leftist songs.

Phil Ochs was perhaps the most polemical of all the singer-songwriters who emerged from the protest song movement of the mid-'60s. As Bob Dylan moved away from the Woody Guthrie tradition, Ochs's material became more topical, focusing on support for the civil-rights movement and opposition to the Vietnam War.

His embrace of these causes was severely tested by the events of 1968; the assassinations of Dr Martin Luther King and Robert Kennedy, followed by the brutal suppression of anti-war protesters at the Democratic Convention in Chicago that year, had a profound effect on Ochs. Having identified so powerfully with the idea that music could change the world, when that turned out to be a false hope he took it personally. He failed to release any more albums after 1970 and took his own life six years later.

This song is based on 'I Dreamed I Saw Joe Hill Last Night', written by Alfred Hayes and Earl Robinson in 1936.

ACCIDENT WAITING TO HAPPEN

There are some people whose politics are based on the assumption that the glass is always half-empty, that the world is out to get them, that everybody is motivated by the same selfish impulses that they themselves are prey to. If you hope to make a better world for everyone, you have to have a degree of trust in humanity.

The Deutsche Demokratische Republik (DDR) was the German name for the former Eastern Bloc state of East Germany.

MOVING THE GOALPOSTS

Gennadi Gerasimov was foreign affairs spokesman for Soviet premier Mikhail Gorbachev during the years of perestroika and glasnost. Witty and urbane, he was markedly different from the standard stodgy Soviet apparatchik, and gave us the first tangible sign that change was coming to Russia.

CINDY OF A THOUSAND LIVES

Cindy Sherman is an American conceptual artist whose work mainly consists of photographs of herself in different roles and costumes. Her early black and white photos purported to be stills from imaginary movies, but in the late '80s she turned to colour, and the images became disturbing, hinting at a macabre underbelly to the American dream.

YOU WOKE UP MY NEIGHBOURHOOD

In April 1991, I was in Washington DC when a friend invited me to look at some drawings by Woody Guthrie that were held at the Smithsonian/Folkways Archive. I had no idea that Woody was an artist, and his sketches really impressed me, particularly one depicting a dancing woman. It was only a few lines of faded watercolour, but it had such life, such joyous motion. Woody had written below the figure 'You Woke Up My Neighborhood'.

A week later I was in Athens, Georgia, to record some songs with REM. When Peter Buck asked me if I had any ideas for a tune that he'd been working up, Woody's title made a pretty good chorus.

TRUST

The sudden appearance of HIV/AIDS in the '80s meant that everyone had to consider the possibility of life-changing consequences every time they had sex with a new partner.

Peter Knowles played for Wolverhampton Wanderers in the late '60s and was a striker in the George Best style. At the height of his career, he announced that he was giving up football to become a Jehovah's Witness.

THE FEW

On a long journey between gigs in Spain, the lyrics of this song began to form in my head. Apart from the driver and myself, everyone else was asleep and my guitar was buried under the luggage at the back of the van. As the images continued to come, I desperately needed a tune to set them to if the moment of inspiration was not to escape me. So in the dark of the van, I began to compose this song to the melody of Bob Dylan's 'Desolation Row'.

When I got to my hotel all I needed to do was to come up with a new tune that had the same metre as Dylan's song.

This lyric concerns the scourge of violent hooliganism and belligerent nationalism displayed by supporters of the England football team at international tournaments in the closing decades of the twentieth century.

The title of the song is a reference to the excuse offered by the football authorities whenever trouble broke out – that it is a minority of fans who behave like this. 'The Few' is also the name that Churchill gave to the RAF pilots who defended England during the Battle of Britain in 1940: 'Never, in the field of human conflict, has so much been owed by so many to so few.'

In recognition of the role that 'Desolation Row' played in the creation of this work, the first four lines are a parody of the opening lines of the eighth verse of Dylan's song. The Baby Brotherhood and the Inter-City Crew were gangs of football hooligans.

The line 'What do they know of England who only England know?' is adapted from 'The English Flag', a poem by Rudyard Kipling published in 1891.

The Empire Stadium was the original name of Wembley Stadium, built for the British Empire Exhibition of 1924.

John Bull is a fictional figure said to be the national personification of Great Britain, in the way that Uncle Sam personifies the USA.

SEXUALITY

None of my uncles ever played for Red Star Belgrade, I don't look anything like Robert De Niro and a Mitsubishi Zero is an aircraft, not a car, and I've never driven one.

Poetic licence is a wonderful thing, but should be used sparingly.

TANK PARK SALUTE

The bombing of Pan Am Flight 103 over Lockerbie in December 1988 was the largest terror attack in British history. I was already an apprehensive flier, and the reports of children's toys and other everyday objects being found in the fields around the village weeks after the event had a deep effect on me. In an attempt to reconcile my feelings, I sat down one night to write a song about the tragedy, utilising a descending tune that I'd worked out on guitar some months before.

Frustratingly, the lyrics weren't really saying anything profound until I came up with the couplet 'I closed my eyes and when I looked / Your name was in the memorial book'. These words took me completely by surprise. Trying to find my way into the mood of the bereaved relatives of the Lockerbie victims, I had unwittingly opened a door to my own bereavement.

My father, Denis Bragg, was diagnosed with terminal lung cancer in July 1975. The doctor in charge of his case suggested that the best way to deal with this devastating news was not to speak about it to my father. As much in shock as anything else, my mother and I followed this advice, to our eternal regret.

When he died fifteen months later, aged fifty-two, we just carried on not speaking about it, not to each other, not to anyone. It became my way of dealing with the grief. Everyone who knew me was aware that I'd lost my father, but no one knew how I felt about it.

When his ashes were interred, Dad's name was written in a large book at the cemetery, open every year on the day that he died. My mother, my brother and I would always visit on the anniversary and go together to view the memorial book. This imagery had somehow bubbled up from my subconscious.

Those two lines caught me unawares and I looked at them on the paper for some while. I thought about turning away from the gravel path that led to the crematorium, back to the safer ground of writing about something that happened to someone else. But my eighteen-year-old self was calling, and I walked beside him again, through the funeral service and the flood of feelings that beset me that day.

And I'm glad I did. The song was written in a cathartic thirty minutes or so and when it was all there on the paper, the spell that had bound me for so many years was broken. I knew that when I played this song live, I would have to talk about what happened to our family when my father died.

So when people tell me that this song helped them to come to terms with the loss of a loved one, I always smile, because it had exactly the same effect on me.

RUMOURS OF WAR

Any hopes that the collapse of the Berlin Wall and the break-up of the Warsaw Pact would herald a period of peace were dashed by the invasion of Iraq in 1990. It's almost as if, having lost an enemy, the West immediately went searching for some new adversary to justify continued arms spending in a post-Cold War environment. This song was written in the lead-up to that conflict.

BODY OF WATER

The involvement of members of the Smiths and REM in the making of *Don't Try This at Home* got my record company very excited. Kicking off with the big, radio-friendly sound of 'Sexuality', they felt this album gave them the opportunity to turn me into a proper pop star who scored regular hit singles. After all, they'd recently got the Housemartins to the top of the charts, why shouldn't they do the same for me?

Early on in the recording process, Johnny Marr and I had written 'Sexuality' together, which he then took back to Manchester and turned into a fabulous monster of a pop song. That set the bar pretty high for the rest of the record and I did my best to create tracks that lived up to Johnny's vision.

On this, the last cut of the album, I felt that we'd made a great record and had every right to finish things off by going completely over the top. Big stomping tune, double-tracked vocals and yes, that's me playing the deranged guitar solo during the fade out. And those lyrics? To be frank, they're nonsense, as was the idea that I could ever become a genuine pop star.

ONTARIO, QUEBEC AND ME

Oh, Canada!

My early records were predominantly sold on vinyl and every single released needed a B-side, which would help sell the record if it wasn't a track that was available elsewhere. With this in mind, I usually cut two or three extra tracks when recording an album. Sometimes, however, you'd go into a studio to make a single and have to come up with a B-side on the spot.

This is one of those songs, written from scratch at Fort Apache Studios in Boston, where I was recording a new version of 'Accident Waiting to Happen' with my band, the Red Stars. We were enjoying the freedom to throw ideas about on the session, and I think that comes across in the performance.

AS LONG AS YOU HOLD ME

I wrote this song for a movie called *Mad Love*, about a young woman with suicidal tendencies. It's based on some words I wrote on hearing of the death of Kurt Cobain. Kirsty MacColl recorded a beautiful version of this song for the movie soundtrack.

FROM RED TO BLUE

This song was the opening track on my first album for five years and, in that period, many things had changed. Prime Minister Thatcher had been deposed, the Cold War was over and, most importantly, I had become someone's dad.

The collapse of the Iron Curtain brought to an end a bloody cycle of European history that had begun in August 1914. The fall of Margaret Thatcher was also a cause for celebration. However, the failure of the Labour party to defeat her successor, John Major, in 1992 broke the hearts of many who had fought so hard against the Tories in the '80s. For others, it signalled that no one cared about collectivism anymore. With communism defeated, they viewed solidarity as an out-of-date idea to be scorned. History had ended, someone declared, and we had won! Break out the champagne – we don't have to pretend to care anymore.

From now on, having a social conscience was for losers. Soon the news stands were full of magazines that celebrated a culture of excess couched in an infantile laddism. Friends who had paid lip service to the cause were to be found eating prawn cocktail sandwiches in private corporate boxes at the football. These people weren't necessarily swapping sides in the debate – they just didn't think that politics really mattered anymore. Style was reasserting its dominance over content and politics was becoming less about principles, more about presentation.

UPFIELD

What was clear from the early '90s was that if the left hoped to hold onto its ideals in the face of such momentous change, we were going to need to find a new way of articulating what we believed in. The language of Marxism, which had framed our discourse for much of the twentieth century, no longer spoke to people about their everyday lives. However, the problems that Marx identified had not been resolved. The term 'socialism' had become tainted by totalitarianism and if we hoped to make a case for a fairer society, we needed to go back to basic principles and create a new language. I've long held that, in order to be effective, socialism has to be a form of organised compassion, like a national health service, free to all at point of use. Socialism without a heart is just hollow dogma.

The imagery of the song is based on an episode in the life of English visionary artist William Blake, who claimed to have seen a tree filled with angels on Peckham Rye as a child.

The Great Wen is a disparaging nickname for London, coined in the 1820s by William Cobbett. A wen is a form of cyst.

BRICKBAT

I was never a believer in Cyril Connolly's dictum that 'there is no more sombre enemy of good art than the pram in the hall', but after our son Jack was born in late 1993, I did wonder if it would have an effect on my songwriting. Connolly may have had a sour view of parenthood, but there is something in what he says, because if the experience of becoming a parent doesn't change your life completely, then you're probably not doing it properly.

I was fortunate in that parenthood changed my life for the better. After ten years on the road, I was ready for a break, so I stopped gigging and became a happy house-daddy. I barely picked up the guitar for a year and when I did I often found that the tunes that I spontaneously strummed bore a strong resemblance to those heard in Jack's favourite, must-watch-it-ten-times-a-day singalong video, *Spider in the Bath*. Eventually, my songwriting instincts reasserted themselves and I wrote 'Brickbat', elated to find that parenthood could be as much of an inspiration as my turbulent singleton years.

The Last Night of the Proms is a concert of patriotic classical music held every year at the Royal Albert Hall in London, accompanied by much jingoistic flag waving.

THE SPACE RACE IS OVER

When I was born in late 1957, the Soviet Union had just fired the first shot of the space race and their duel with the United States illuminated my childhood. Each new mission was marked in my school books with numerous drawings of astronauts and cosmonauts circling the earth.

When our son was born, the first word he learned to say after 'mama' and 'dada' was 'moon'. Before he could walk, he could point to the bright sphere in the night sky and identify it by name. It reminded me of my own childhood infatuation with our nearest astral neighbour and inspired me to write this song.

THE FOURTEENTH OF FEBRUARY

I wrote this on Valentine's Day 1995. I was in the studio that day, recording *William Bloke*, and on the way there I came up with some lyrics that fitted nicely to a tune that I'd composed while playing guitar to amuse Jack. That morning my partner, Juliet, gave me a book of love poems in which she had marked a particular work: 'I Wish I Could Remember That First Day' by Christina Rossetti. It was a fitting choice as neither of us had much recollection of the first time that we met, some eight years before we got together as a couple.

KING JAMES VERSION

Florence Ballard, one of the founding members of the Supremes, struggled with alcoholism and depression, dying in poverty in 1976 aged thirty-two.

THE BOY DONE GOOD

Football references were all the rage when laddism took hold in the early '90s, and metaphors about the beautiful game had often peppered my love songs. When Johnny Marr offered me this tune, I decided to collect up all the ones I had knocking about in my notebooks and string them together in this lyric.

In medieval Europe, there were no weekends – workers toiled every day of the week except Sunday, the Sabbath. Along with the Christian festivals of Easter, Whitsun and Christmas, workers could also expect to have a day off on the feast day of a saint with a local or occupational connection. These days seldom ran consecutively, so there were very few weekend-style breaks in the work cycle.

In order to enjoy a two-day break, factory workers in nineteenth-century Britain began staying at home on the first day of the week, claiming they were celebrating the feast of St Monday. This initiative marked the beginning of the struggle for the five-day week.

ENGLAND, HALF ENGLISH

Colin MacInnes's sharp observations of the changes wrought in '50s England by the influx of West Indian immigrants and American pop culture reveal him to be nothing less than the hip George Orwell. Unlike most commentators of the time, MacInnes welcomed these new arrivals and celebrated them in novels such as *Absolute Beginners* and *Mr Love & Justice*.

In December 1957, he wrote an article about the first English pop star, Tommy Steele, entitled 'Young England, Half English', in which he recognised that Steele's audience, wearing foreign-style clothes, drinking foreign pop and listening to a foreign music were not nearly as English as their parents were, at least in terms of culture. The idea that each generation modifies national identity by adding new cultural dimensions, often borrowed from overseas, ran contrary to the tradition-alist notion that Englishness was a static, narrowly defined construct.

The band that was backing me at the time, referred to collectively as the Blokes, had a long pedigree of playing world music. They provided me with the ideal setting for a song that explored this issue. During a soundcheck, they were jamming an Algerian folk song, the chorus of which translated as 'Oh my country, oh my country, what a beautiful country you are' – the band sing the original Arabic between verses ('Le-li Umma le-li-ya, bledi g'desh akh!'). I borrowed that tune and wrote this song.

Essex Man is a term used to describe a stereotypical working class rightwinger, of the sort who voted for Margaret Thatcher. I was born in Essex.

Marmite is the brand name of a savoury spread made from yeast left over from the process of brewing beer. Its popularity is largely confined to the British Isles and, even here, people tend to love it or hate it. Soldiers are thin strips of toast that can be dipped into the top of a soft-boiled egg.

Bubble 'n' squeak is a Cockney speciality, consisting of left-over vegetables from yesterday's dinner, traditionally potatoes and cabbage, mixed together and pan-fried.

Morris dancing is a form of traditional English dance for men involving bells, hankies and flower-decked hats.

The three lions on the badge of the England football team come originally from the arms of William of Normandy, who conquered England in 1066.

NPWA

Over the past thirty years, globalisation has made it possible for companies to place themselves beyond the reach of tax regimes while moving production to countries where workers have few rights. As a result, governments and unions have increasingly found it difficult to hold corporations to account. At the same time, supranational financial institutions such as the World Bank, the International Monetary Fund (IMF) and the World Trade Organization (WTO) have sought to speed this process up by insisting on the privatisation of public services.

In recent years, those who believe that people should be more important than profits have come together to protest against economic decisions being made behind closed doors.

TAKE DOWN THE UNION JACK

Modern Britain is a highly centralised state. Power and the ability to wield it are jealously guarded by the Westminster Parliament. While some powers have been devolved to the Scots and the Welsh, no arrangements have been made for giving power to the English.

Part of the problem is the ambiguous nature of the English identity. Without a border between themselves and Westminster, the English have difficulty working out where Britishness ends and Englishness begins. Devolution has inspired the people of Scotland to reimagine themselves as a confident, outward-looking nation. Meanwhile, England continues to dream about the British Empire and the Second World War, while spending money to keep up the pretence of being a world power.

The British state came into being just over 300 years ago and, in each century, the nations that make up its constituent parts have changed. It looks likely that this century will also ring changes. Scottish independence just might be the wake-up call that the English sorely need.

Gilbert and George are conceptual artists who live in London. Their recent works feature Union Jacks and naked pictures of themselves.

TEARS OF MY TRACKS

During the recording of *England, Half English* I went to a Sunday boot sale with Ben Mandelson, my guitar player.

We found a stall with loads of seven-inch singles and, to our delight, they were mostly records that were big during our schooldays. We kept pulling out the classic ones and saying to one another 'Remember this?'

Gradually, it dawned on me that these weren't just a random bunch of old records for sale; this was clearly someone's personal collection, once the centre of their teenage universe. We were rummaging through the adolescence of Minky Mac-Muffin, her name written in biro on every sleeve.*

I looked up at the vendor; she was a pale, winnowy woman about the same age as me. 'Are you Minky MacMuffin?' I asked hesitantly.

'Yes' she said, turning her head away from my gaze and biting her lip. Ben and I pretended to carry on looking at the records in the box, but both of us knew we'd be buying no vinyl here.

YARRA SONG

The Yarra is the river the runs through Melbourne. When I first toured Australia in 1987, my agent hailed from the city, as did my support band, the wonderful Weddings, Parties, Anything. As a result, something of the place rubbed off on me. It's a temperate city in a very hot land and, as is mentioned in the song, the fact that they provide a brolly – an umbrella – in your hotel room somehow makes me feel at home.

Flinders Street runs parallel with the Yarra through the centre of the city.

'That funny game they play' is a reference to Australian Rules Football, first played in Melbourne in 1859. To say it's a full contact sport doesn't really capture the enthusiasm with which its players come into contact with each other.

---

* Names have been changed to protect those involved.

The Saints is the nickname of St Kilda, one of nine professional Aussie Rules teams from the Melbourne area. The Magpies are their deadly rivals, Collingwood.

'Barracking' is Australian slang for supporting.

Sunday Too Far Away is an Australian movie about a group of itinerant sheep shearers in the Outback who go on strike.

The Hammers is the nickname of West Ham United, the football team from East London that I support. 'I'm Forever Blowing Bubbles' is their anthem.

OLD CLASH FAN FIGHT SONG

Although our bondage trousers no longer fit us, those of us who were touched by the fire of punk still find ways to hang onto that DIY attitude.

I KEEP FAITH

As far as I'm concerned, the best kind of Billy Bragg songs are both personal and political. 'I Keep Faith' is a good example. Depending on how I introduce this song, it can be either a song of personal commitment or a collective call to arms.

M FOR ME

While most love songs concern themselves with the euphoria of newly found love, one of the great challenges in life is how to maintain a long-term relationship with those we love the most.

SOMETHING HAPPENED

Sometimes you just have to say it plain.

JANUARY SONG

In the first month of 2012, I headed to Los Angeles to make a new album under the encouraging eye of my friend Joe Henry. For many reasons, it felt as if I was making a new start, having lived through a time of great changes, both personally and professionally. This song, written and recorded on the final day of the sessions, seemed to sum up my sense that, after a period of things coming to an end, I was now moving into a world of new beginnings and exciting possibilities.

HANDYMAN BLUES

There is an old saying that states, 'To a man with a hammer in his hand, everything looks like a nail.' For some us, that nail will never go in straight, no matter how many times we hit it.

DO UNTO OTHERS

In 2011, I was invited to contribute a song to a project marking the 400th anniversary of the King James Bible. Sixty-six artists were each asked to write a performance piece based on one of the books of the Bible. 'Send me one from the New Testament,' I told the director when he asked me to choose a book 'You know, one of the books where Jesus is being a socialist.'

He sent me the Book of Luke, which contains the verse, 'Do unto others as you would have them do to you.' Or as the King James Version has it: 'And as ye would that men should do to you, do ye also to them likewise.' That didn't scan quite so well, so I went with the New International Version.

GOODBYE, GOODBYE

In March 2007, comedian Phill Jupitus invited me to be a guest on his final radio show for BBC 6 Music, where he'd been the breakfast DJ since its inception. As a special treat, the show was to be broadcast from the kitchen of his home in Leigh-on-Sea in Essex. As it was an early start, I spent the night before in his spare bedroom, which was fine until, at 7 a.m., I was blasted out of bed by him kicking off the show.

I stumbled downstairs to be greeted with a kitchen full of his family and friends, and the news that I wasn't due on air for two hours. I'm not much of a morning person, so I grabbed a mug of coffee and a slice of toast, and went to ease myself into the day in the empty living room. Propped up in the corner was Phill's brand new Taylor acoustic guitar.

It's a widely held belief among singer-songwriters that new guitars always have songs in them and, picking it up, I found my hands playing these lovely descending chords. In no time at all, I'd written this song of parting. When I performed it live on air, an hour or so later, it was the very first time that anyone other than myself had heard the song.

TOMORROW'S GOING TO BE A BETTER DAY

The changes that have occurred in the record industry since I started writing songs forty years ago are immense. In the late '70s, the Sex Pistols and the Clash were playing regular gigs in the city where I lived, but I had to rely on the weekly music press to find out about them and, unless John Peel played them on his late night radio show, I had no way of hearing their music. And if I wanted to express my views, as a nineteen-year-old with no qualifications, I had little choice but to learn to play guitar, write some songs and negotiate a path via the *NME* and the BBC.

The Internet has changed all that, and for the better. Instead of having to read about music that doesn't interest you in the weekly press, you can now set your own preferences to receive news about your favourite artists or explore musical genres beyond the confines of the mainstream.

The most empowering aspect of this new age of information is that everyone can make a contribution to the debate, democratising the formation of opinion. If you're trying to offer an original perspective of the world by joining the dots in a different way to everybody else, you have more dots than ever to play with and multiple angles on them.

But this democratisation is a double-edged sword: information technology empowers the pessimists as well as the optimists, and there will always be those who feel empowered by drawing a penis on every pretty picture they find.

Confronted by the darker side of humanity that has been revealed by the truthful mirror of social media, I've come to the conclusion that the real enemy of those of us who want to create a better world is not capitalism or conservatism, but cynicism: the dogged belief that nothing will ever change for the better, that everybody is only in it for themselves and that no one cares about this stuff anyway. I'm out to prove that idea wrong with every line I write.

SONG OF THE ICEBERG

When I was approached to write a song to mark the 100th anniversary of the sinking of the *Titanic* in 2012, I was immediately struck by the problem of how to bring a fresh angle to a story with which everyone was familiar. Half-joking, I suggested to the producer that I might write a song from the perspective of the iceberg that sank the ship. He thought it was a great idea, and so I started to consider the journey that the iceberg was on, a continual cycle of transformation and movement that lasted millennia. The principle behind the song is one that serves as perhaps the best justification for creating any kind of art – the urge to articulate something from a different perspective, one that you don't see reflected anywhere else.

Index of Titles and First Lines

titles are in italics